4/05

dyo

6/05

MOLLY E. HOLZSCHLAG

design your own:

creating and promoting successful small business sites

AVA Publishing SA
Switzerland

Sterling Publishing Co., Inc.
New York

AN AVA BOOK
PUBLISHED BY AVA PUBLISHING SA
c/o Fidinter SA
Ch. de la Joliette 2
Case postale 96
1000 Lausanne 6
Switzerland
Tel: +41 786 005 109
Email: enquiries@avabooks.ch

DISTRIBUTED BY THAMES AND HUDSON (EX-NORTH AMERICA)
181a High Holborn
London WC1V 7QX
United Kingdom
Tel: +44 20 7845 5000
Fax: +44 20 7845 5055
Email: sales@thameshudson.co.uk
thamesandhudson.com

DISTRIBUTED BY STERLING
PUBLISHING CO., INC.
IN THE USA
387 Park Avenue South
New York, NY 10016-8810
Tel: +1 212 532 7160
Fax: +1 212 213 2495
sterlingpub.com

IN CANADA
Sterling Publishing
c/o Canadian Manda Group
One Atlantic Avenue, Suite 105
Toronto, Ontario M6K 3E7

ENGLISH LANGUAGE SUPPORT OFFICE
AVA Publishing (UK) Ltd.
Tel: +44 1903 204 455
Email: enquiries@avabooks.co.uk

ISBN 2-88479-021-7

10 9 8 7 6 5 4 3 2 1

Design by **Gavin Ambrose**
Email: gavin@dircon.co.uk

Production and separations by **AVA Book Production Pte. Ltd.**, Singapore
Tel: +65 6334 8173
Fax: +65 6334 0752
Email: production@avabooks.com.sg

ACKNOWLEDGEMENTS

▶

No book is a solitary activity, and while the author gets much credit, there are many people who are seminal to a book's realisation. I'd like to take the opportunity to thank them here.

My editor, Natalia Price-Cabrera, is a wonderful editor who helps refine my idea with a subtle but effective hand. She is also patient and kind, two qualities that make working with her a joy. Brian Morris, AVA's publisher, is a uniquely generous and warm individual for whom it is an honour to work. I'd also like to thank Laura Owen, Assistant Editor at AVA, who helped out with many details and Gavin Ambrose for his design of the book.

My love and gratitude to Michael Forkan. He provides constancy, creative influence, and enthusiastic support of my writing. My mother, stepfather, and brothers are not only the foundational source of strength in my life, but also of artistic inspiration via a shared passion for art, architecture, literature, music, self-expression, and beauty.

Finally, I am most thankful to my readers, website visitors, and the many people whom I get to meet at conferences and events. It is you who make it possible for me to continue doing work that is both challenging and greatly rewarding.

SLEAZENATION.COM

Hello, and welcome to sleazenation.com.

Trainspotters will be salivating over our 75th edition on sale now... clocking in with over 128 pages of cutting-edge music, fresh fashion, photodocumentary elegance and round the world trips. While other mags have brightened up for summer, we're the one's with the black cover.

Highlights include the return of Sleaze snapper of olde, Ewen Spencer, who has teamed up with Polly Banks for a 10 page feast of mid summer fashion.

Travel is the theme and we get lost in the ex-most dangerous city in the world, Beirut, with author Kris Kenway. Check out the website's exclusive guide courtesy of Sleaze Folk's Clotaire K.

Next stop is Berlin where we go clubbing on watermelon cocktails before popping into Monaco for beauty treatments with D List celebs. To counteract the fluff, two UK activists give us the lowdown on dodging bullets in The Gaza Strip.

If all that globetrotting's got your head spinning, get EXTREEEEME! with Stuart Turnbull's six page whirl around British fairgrounds. Neil Massey's pics aren't bad either.

BEIRUT GUIDE

CONTACT

SUBSCRIBE

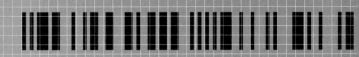

CONTENTS

HOW TO GET THE MOST OUT OF THIS BOOK

Divided into four chapters, this book sets out how to design your own online storefront. The DYO series is purposely meant to be visually appealing, content-rich, and very easy to use. Take a moment to see the various features used to assist you in getting to the information you need – and fast!

The Text
The concise and instructional text is written in an energetic style to guide readers through the process.

Images
Screenshots of actual websites are used, along with their website addresses, to provide ideas and inspiration.

ALL ABOUT PERSONAS

In the last few years the concept of personas has arisen in professional web circles. Personas are the creation of fictitious audience members that are then used to test sites for usability. Essentially, these fictitious personalities are matched with aspects of the site: Language, colours, content, and navigation – to gain insight on how a given person might respond to a particular aspect of the site's design or interactive features.

Creating personas can be effective for the small business storefront owner wishing to work through how site visitors might use their website. You can create a persona simply by writing a profile of the fictitious audience member:

Sandra. Sandra is 65 years old and has recently retired from a long-term career as a schoolteacher. She has excellent retirement benefits and has also made some very good investments in both the stock market and real estate. She is a widow with grown-up children, and is interested in finding a good lawyer to help her plan her estate accordingly.

NOTE
Depending upon how your server situation is set up, you may be able to look at the server logs. These logs can help a great deal when figuring out where people are coming from, what kind of technologies they're using, and so forth. This information will help shape your site for the future.

While definitions of the kind described here are preliminary and can really only be used as a gauge of what your real audience will be like, they do provide an excellent starting point. You will have to be vigilant to see how things progress once your site is up and running. At that point, you can ask for regular feedback from your site visitors, which will be very helpful in terms of clarifying how successful your site is, and how you might have to modify what you're doing to stay on track.

1.6 Examples of the wealth of data available on most server logs.
AWSTATS.SOURCEFORGE.NET

DESIGN YOUR OWN: E-SHOP

26 27

DESIGNING YOUR SITE

Tips & Notes
Useful tips and notes are used throughout the book to provide interesting insights and additional information.

Captions
Website addresses are listed of all screenshots shown for easy reference.

1

Whether you are using your site to promote a business or to sell a product, the site must contain features that put your visitors at ease and help them get to the information or products they require with as few steps as possible.

One of the first rules of design is to know your audience. Another rule is to know yourself! Figuring out audience and business goals is the primary step in creating a successful business relationship. By ensuring your visitors know they are welcome and clearly stating the goals of the site, the potential for a long-term relationship takes root. This chapter starts out by helping you get a handle on this important aspect of the website/web-visitor relationship. You'll explore the concept of personas, examine your business goals, and undertake several tasks that will help you clarify this all-important foundation for your site.

'THE SUCCESS OF A STOREFRONT WEBSITE LIES MOSTLY IN YOUR ABILITY TO CREATE A COMFORTABLE AND EASY RELATIONSHIP WITH YOUR SITE VISITORS.'

4

While learning to customise your site for its audience, adding a merchant account, and adding a shopping cart are all important aspects of putting together a great e-shop, adding promotions and marketing are a necessary part of your site's success.

Whether you intend to use your website as an addition to your offline business, to provide products or services, or as a forum for your expression, you have to put some effort into marketing it. With the millions of Web pages available today, your content could be lost and, as great as your site is, it might never get seen.

WITH THE MILLIONS OF WEB PAGES AVAILABLE TODAY, YOUR WEB SITE MUST BE MARKETED EFFECTIVELY IN ORDER TO STAND OUT.

Sample Source Code
Actual HTML source code is used whenever possible to provide real-life examples and solutions.

Examples
Screenshots of actual program interfaces are shown to familiarise readers.

Changing Colours & Fonts

If you don't like the colours and fonts for the template, you can make changes in the style sheet file. This is the file that ends in .css. Open up the file in your editor and consider the following code:

```
body {
        font-family: Arial, Helvetica, sans-serif;
        font-size: 16px;
        line-height: 22px;
        color: #660000;
        background-color: #FFFFFF;
}
a:link {
        font-family: Arial, Helvetica, sans-serif;
        font-size: 16px;
        color: #666633;
        text-decoration: none;
}
a:visited {
        font-family: Arial, Helvetica, sans-serif;
        font-size: 16px;
        color: #999933;
        text-decoration: none;
}
a:active {
        font-family: Arial, Helvetica, sans-serif;
        font-size: 16px;
        color: #996633;
        text-decoration: none;
}
a:hover {
        font-family: Arial, Helvetica, sans-serif;
        font-size: 16px;
        color: #660000;
        text-decoration: underline;
}
```

To change colours, simply find the hexadecimal equivalent of the colour you'd like for each feature described in the style sheet, and replace it.

000000	003300	006600	009900	00CC00	00FF00
000033	003333	006633	009933	00CC33	00FF33
000066	003366	006666	009966	00CC66	00FF66
000099	003399	006699	009999	00CC99	00FF99
0000CC	0033CC	0066CC	0099CC	00CCCC	00FFCC
0000FF	0033FF	0066FF	0099FF	00CCFF	00FFFF
330000	333300	336600	339900	33CC00	33FF00
330033	333333	336633	339933	33CC33	33FF33
330066	333366	336666	339966	33CC66	33FF66
330099	333399	336699	339999	33CC99	33FF99
3300CC	3333CC	3366CC	3399CC	33CCCC	33FFCC
3300FF	3333FF	3366FF	3399FF	33CCFF	33FFFF
660000	663300	666600	669900	66CC00	66FF00
660033	663333	666633	669933	66CC33	66FF33
660066	663366	666666	669966	66CC66	66FF66
660099	663399	666699	669999	66CC99	66FF99
6600CC	6633CC	6666CC	6699CC	66CCCC	66FFCC
6600FF	6633FF	6666FF	6699FF	66CCFF	66FFFF
990000	993300	996600	999900	99CC00	99FF00
990033	993333	996633	999933	99CC33	99FF33
990066	993366	996666	999966	99CC66	99FF66
990099	993399	996699	999999	99CC99	99FF99
9900CC	9933CC	9966CC	9999CC	99CCCC	99FFCC
9900FF	9933FF	9966FF	9999FF	99CCFF	99FFFF
CC0000	CC3300	CC6600	CC9900	CCCC00	CCFF00
CC0033	CC3333	CC6633	CC9933	CCCC33	CCFF33
CC0066	CC3366	CC6666	CC9966	CCCC66	CCFF66
CC0099	CC3399	CC6699	CC9999	CCCC99	CCFF99
CC00CC	CC33CC	CC66CC	CC99CC	CCCCCC	CCFFCC
CC00FF	CC33FF	CC66FF	CC99FF	CCCCFF	CCFFFF
FF0000	FF3300	FF6600	FF9900	FFCC00	FFFF00
FF0033	FF3333	FF6633	FF9933	FFCC33	FFFF33
FF0066	FF3366	FF6666	FF9966	FFCC66	FFFF66
FF0099	FF3399	FF6699	FF9999	FFCC99	FFFF99
FF00CC	FF33CC	FF66CC	FF99CC	FFCCCC	FFFFCC
FF00FF	FF33FF	FF66FF	FF99FF	FFCCFF	FFFFFF

1.15 The above hexadecimal chart can be found at molly.com/molly/webdesign/ colorchart.html.

Sidebars
Sidebars are used to draw out specific issues related to the text and provide additional information.

Navigation
Page numbers and chapter headings are located on coloured side bars for easy reference.

INTRODUCTION

Using the web for doing business has been part of the web's framework since its very first days. Companies such as CD-Now (cdnow.com) had already been putting together a strategy to sell via the Internet. At that point, they were using technologies other than the web, so when the web became available, it proved to be a good platform for commercial ideas.

But of course there were many limitations and have been problems along the way. Anyone who promises you that you can make a million bucks online simply by slapping up a website is out of line. No one can promise that kind of success. But, you can realistically look at the issues and then decide for yourself how to best tackle the problems.

Remember that the web is very young. In the early days, a lot depended upon the savvy of the designers of websites to figure out how to make them more interesting and interactive than a printed brochure.

And, while the various technologies it embodies are getting richer and more accessible to the common man and woman, figuring out not only how to create a website but much less make it work effectively within those limitations remains a difficult task.

But those are the things that can be taught, and will be taught, in this book. You'll learn about designing for your customers, learn about merchant accounts for online transactions, read about hosted and out-of-box style solutions. You'll learn about how to add a shopping cart to your site – whether the site is new or has been around for some time and you're ready to offer products. Finally, you'll learn about promoting your site, which may prove to be the real essence of your site's potential growth in the long run.

What about the things that can't really be taught? For example, you know your audience and product much better than I do. And if you don't, you should! After all, people aren't going to come to a site that has nothing to offer. Well, they might drop by, but will they stay, explore, purchase? If there's nothing there to meet their needs, they'll find somewhere else to go.

Readers are going to be familiar with the large, international retailers such as Amazon and eBay. People know about these services because they were in the game early, and first and foremost, have figured out the answer to the magic question of how to fulfil a customer's needs. Their names have become web brands, and that is how they have built both a critical mass of users and services; not to mention the technology that addresses their needs as easily and simply as possible.

Porter Glendinning, a web/UI "commando" for Commerce One who also runs his own web development company, Cerebellion Design, supports the idea that answering need is a crucial early piece of a website's commercial success. "People shop on the web because it provides them with something that other outlets don't," he says, "convenience, cost savings, easier price comparisons, and so on."

So you, as the person with the commercial site idea, must be able to provide those things to your audience. That's the first step. What does your customer need and how can you effectively supply it? Answer that question successfully, and you begin the road to an equally successful online business.

Once you've answered that question, the challenge becomes getting the people to your site. This can be a very difficult task, because there is no clear-cut way to get there. Various marketing pundits have set forth ideas such as using aggressive "guerrilla" style marketing campaigns, and almost everyone who has ever surfed the web has wondered about the success of annoying pop-up ads. There is no question that driving traffic becomes a paramount concern.

For the established business, it might be easier to achieve interest because there are built-in advertising and marketing plans in place. The website should then be made as much a part of these existing plans as possible, and worked into future plans and budgets as well. This ensures you have the ideas and resources to use your existing marketing means to carry the message about your online services.

For the new company, whether large, medium, or just a "mom 'n' pop" style shop, the task is more difficult. And, the economic shifts within the Internet industry specifically and the world at large aren't making it easier for the smaller guy and girl to be seen.

You have to figure out a way to get the name and idea out there, you have to have an angle. But, points out Glendinning, "it's not enough to be clever. I think it's only going to get harder for newcomers to get eyeballs unless they're really doing something new, or better... you have to offer a better service, a cheaper product – some sort of incentive to pull people away from that big, recognised name that's doing the same or a similar thing."

Pulling off a successful storefront on the web is a commitment in the same way any business is a commitment. I highly recommend that if you are just starting out as a new business, you consider the two important questions raised in this introduction. If you have good, solid answers and a confident plan, read on! If not, I recommend taking an hour and listing out your business goals. This will at least give you the framework for working through your ideas, and hopefully be ready to meet any challenges that arise with savvy.

Tapping into the fun and functionality of the web is going to be a large part of your job as a person striking out to make a storefront website successful. What you'll learn in this book will be about solving problems by beginning simply and building from there. What you learn from time spent evaluating your own business goals will be inherently attached to your success.

> " It's not enough to be clever. I think it's only going to get harder for newcomers to get eyeballs unless they're really doing something new, or better..."

– **Porter Glendinning** Cerebellion Design

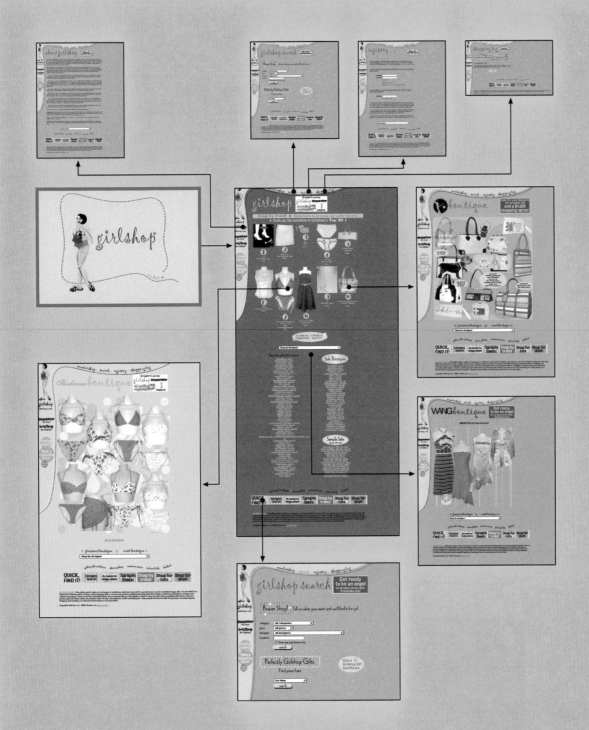

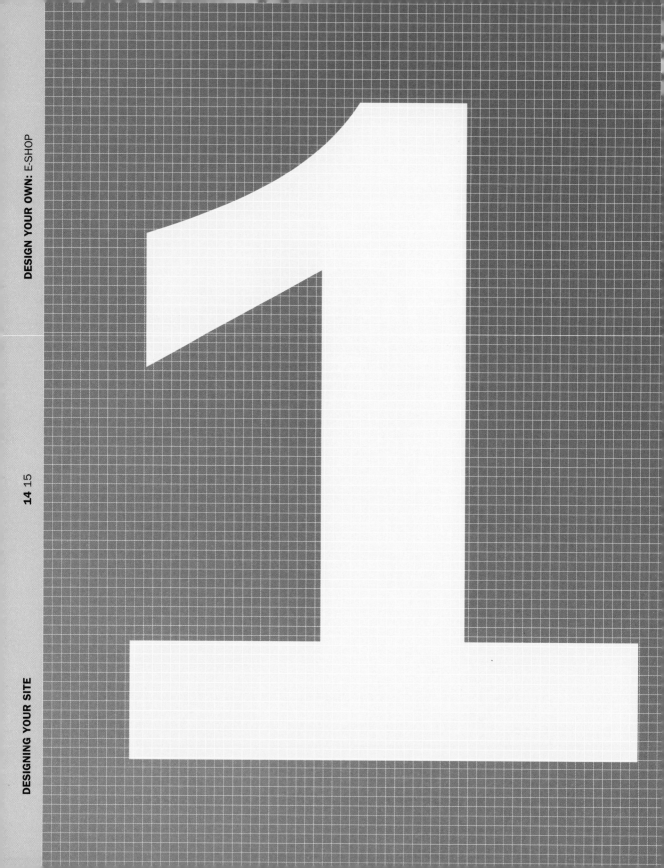

DESIGNING YOUR SITE

Whether you are using your site to promote a business or to sell a product, the site must contain features that put your visitors at ease and help them get to the information or products they require with as few steps as possible.

One of the first rules of design is to know your audience. Another rule is to know yourself! Figuring out audience and business goals is the primary step to creating a successful business relationship. By ensuring your visitors know they are welcome and clearly stating the goals of the site, the potential for a long-term relationship takes root. This chapter starts out by helping you get a handle on this important aspect of the website/web-visitor relationship. You'll explore the concept of personas, examine your business goals, and undertake several tasks that will help you clarify this all-important foundation for your site.

"THE SUCCESS OF A STOREFRONT WEBSITE LIES MOSTLY IN YOUR ABILITY TO CREATE A COMFORTABLE AND EASY RELATIONSHIP WITH YOUR SITE VISITORS."

▶

The most important idea to keep in your mind when approaching the task of designing your storefront is to work with the people you wish to serve and not against them. This means examining aspects of human life and responding to those aspects. Such traits include the way we think, the way our memories work, how our bodies respond, how – and why – we may perceive images in a certain way, and our emotional response to our environment. It is your job as the creator of the site to see to it that these issues are taken into consideration before you attempt your design. You'll read tips and insights throughout this chapter that will help you think about the kinds of people that might be visiting you online, and how you can best reach out to them in a personal and lasting way.

With an awareness of audience and business goals, you can then move on to create a website that addresses these concerns. You'll create a site in this chapter that promotes a small legal business. The site involves providing information about the business and the services it offers – which in this instance aren't online services. Rather, the site exists as a means to encourage potential clients to contact the lawyer.

In creating this first site, you'll learn to put your best face forward and provide quick, easy access to information about your business and its services. Later in the book, you'll design a sales-oriented site with the intention to get people to your products and ultimately purchase those products using the tools you provide.

Good relationships are based on caring. Great relationships are based on love. Love your audience! That means caring for them as you would yourself. But how is this relationship achieved? And how does it turn into a functional website?

Organisation and planning, that's how! By getting your ideas organised, exploring the potential audience for your site, clearly stating your business goals, and having a plan in place, you can achieve the headier goal of having a great relationship with your customers.

1.1 Sample websites selling merchandise for children range from the sweet and whimsical to bold and vibrant. Sites pictured opposite include (top to bottom): **SMILECHILD.CO.UK**, **BOYSSTUFF.CO.UK**, **GROWGROWGROW.COM**, **POPCORNLIVE.CO.UK**.

1.1

1.2

1.2 The designs of retail stores can really run the gamut, as these examples illustrate. OREGANOS.COM, CHOOCHLAND.COM, KRISPYKREME.COM, SCARYSTORIES.COM, FOSSIL.COM, SEPHORA.COM, BILLABONG.COM, JIMMYJOHNS.COM, BLUEFLY.COM, BUFFALOEXCHANGE.COM, ANNASUI.COM and FREEBORD.COM.

Writing a Business Plan

A very important step in developing a business is to write a business plan. Business plans typically detail the short- and long-term goals of your business, how your business will be financed, what competition your business faces, and what kind of business it will be (corporation, sole-proprietorship, etc.).

The U.S. Small Business Administration (SBA) has an excellent online guide that will be helpful to business owners worldwide who would like to create a business plan: SBA.GOV/STARTING/INDEXBUSPLANS.HTML. There are also excellent software tools such as financial calculators and business planning productivity kits available in stores and online. An excellent resource for business planning in general is Bplans.com, which also provides sections on website plans that can help you create a plan especially for your website, BPLANS.COM.

If you've ever put together a home page, you'll find planning a storefront website is exactly like planning that kind of project. If you've never worked on a website, think about projects you might organise at home: designing the garden, rearranging a room, tiling a floor. Just as each of these tasks is easier to achieve with a little planning, so will your site's goals be easier to address once you define your goals.

In order to better establish a great relationship with your site's customers, you'll want to ask some very important questions:

What is the
intention
of your site?

TIP

Many professional website designers keep meticulous documentation regarding audience and site goals. Since your website and its customers may well change over time, it's a very good idea to have some kind of permanent record of these changes, allowing you to analyse the growth of your site and prepare for future needs.

Who is the
audience
for your site?

What are your ultimate
goals
with the site?

In the following sections, you'll work through some tasks to help you clarify these important early steps in the development of your storefront website.

What is Your Intent?

"mission s

Intention in this context refers to coming to a clear decision about what you'd like to use your web page for: To promote, to sell, to provide customer service, or all of these things. This doesn't necessarily mean that what you decide today about your site is going to be the way the site grows and changes – websites are, after all, living and growing entities.

Remember an exercise in school called free writing?
One very helpful way to get organised is to write out lists of your thoughts and ideas about your site and its goals. Grab an old-fashioned pen and paper. If you prefer, you can certainly open up a text editor on your computer such as Notepad (Window) or SimpleText (Mac) and get ready to type away.

Quickly write or type any words that describe the goals of your website. Don't think about this part of the list – be creative! Just go fast and see what you come up with. Then, study the resulting list, and see if all the ideas you have for your site are really what you want to be doing with the site. Now, you'll gather your ideas into a more formal, one-paragraph mission statement. In this statement, clearly state the real intent of the site.

1.3 Professional, elegant, yet simply designed legal sites instil confidence in potential clients, **INSULLAW.COM**.
1.4 Music sites tend to be wilder, with edgier designs appealing to younger audiences, **EMINEM.COM**.

atements"

Here are some examples:

" The intent of my site is to promote my legal services to the members of my local community. The site provides a description of my services and specialty in the area of estate law, information about my education, background, and interests, and complete contact information for potential clients to get in touch."

1.3

" I want to promote my rap group to audiences worldwide. The site will have a discography, lyrics, bio information on the band members, tour dates, and plenty of downloadable audio and video samples."

1.4

◀◀

"The intent of my site is to sell fine, expensive teas. The emphasis is on product quality, with the goal of providing plenty of unique information about various teas from around the world, introducing my customers to new flavours as well as new ideas. The company ships internationally, and provides excellent customer service via the storefront site."

Try it out for yourself! Once you're done, you're ready to think about who will be visiting your site.

1.5

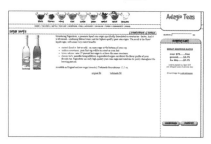

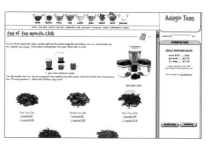

TIP

Look online for websites that are providing similar services or products to those you'd like to offer. Notice which designs appeal to you, and whether the sites clearly express their intent. Model your own content on the successful sites you find.

1.5 Adagio Teas does an excellent job of appealing to customers with its easy-to-use interface and relaxed design, **ADAGIO.COM.**

Defining Your Audience

Figuring out who the audience is for your storefront website can often be done through your mission statement. If you examine the sample statements from the last exercise, you'll find that some idea of who your potential customers might be lies right in the description of your intent.

First consider the case of the lawyer who wishes to promote her legal services. In that case description the services are going to be provided to local customers interested in estate-related legal assistance. There's a lot of information there if you look below the surface: One can imagine that many older people will be seeking out such services, and that the general economic level of clients will be middle class or higher. Understanding these subtleties can in turn assist you when designing your site – knowing you potentially have many older clients means high contrast colours with fonts that are easy to read. Clients with more money might be attracted to a more elegant presentation than one that is more friendly or direct.

For our rap group example, we know the audience is going to be younger and broader in scope than our first example. This information allows you to think about a flashier, edgier design that will appeal to younger people. Finally, our fine tea example demonstrates the need for a sophisticated approach for a worldwide audience of young professionals and more mature individuals with plenty of money to spend on the finer details in life.

All About Personas

In the last few years the concept of personas has arisen in professional web circles. Personas are the creation of fictitious audience members that are then used to test sites for usability. Essentially, these fictitious personalities are matched with aspects of the site: Language, colours, content, and navigation – to gain insight on how a given person might respond to a particular aspect of the site's design or interactive features.

Creating personas can be effective for the small business storefront owner wishing to work through how site visitors might use their website. You can create a persona simply by writing a profile of the fictitious audience member:

Sandra. Sandra is 65 years old and has recently retired from a long-term career as a schoolteacher. She has excellent retirement benefits and has also made some very good investments in both the stock market and real estate. She is a widow with grown-up children, and is interested in finding a good lawyer to help her plan her estate accordingly.

> **NOTE**
>
> Depending upon how your server situation is set up, you may be able to look at the server logs. These logs can help a great deal when figuring out where people are coming from, what kind of technologies they're using, and so forth. This information will help shape your site for the future.

While definitions of the kind described here are preliminary and can really only be used as a gauge of what your real audience will be like, they do provide an excellent starting point. You will have to be vigilant to see how things progress once your site is up and running. At that point, you can ask for regular feedback from your site visitors, which will be very helpful in terms of clarifying how successful your site is, and how you might have to modify what you're doing to stay on track.

1.6

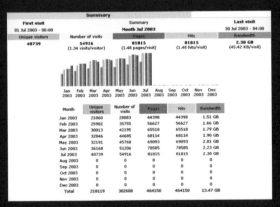

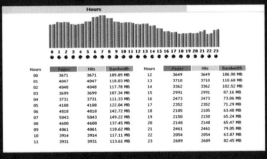

1.6 Examples of the wealth of data available on most server logs, **AWSTATS.SOURCEFORGE.NET**.

Defining Goals

▶

If this sounds a lot like defining the intent of the site, that's because the process is related to it. But, the real concern with this process is to look at what you want to do after you understand your desired intent and the potential audience for your site.

To help evaluate goals for your storefront, do the following:

– Study your original statement of intent. Ask and answer the following question: Do the original intent and the audience response match up?

– Examine any audience personas you might have created. Do you feel they accurately represent the kinds of people you want to be producing your site for?

– Answer the following questions: How do you see your site six months from now? A year? Two years?

Your answers here don't have to be incredibly long. Hone in specifically on what you really want to do in the short run, for your audience, and looking to the future.

If your answers to the first two questions are positive, you are on the right track! If not, you may have to go back and refine your original idea a bit more and possibly refine your personas.

For the third question, the answers are going to be very specific. More than anything, it's a great exercise to write answers to these more theoretical questions because you'll gain a good idea into what might work effectively for you over time, and what might not.

Save your document somewhere safe, so you can return to it later on for re-evaluation.

1.7

   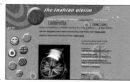

1.7 Screenshots from **LETSGORETRO.COM**.

STUDY

EXAMINE

ANSWER

City Lights Booksellers

▶

The City Lights website first began as a means of telling people about the history of the bookseller, to announce meetings, and to let people know what books they publish. Now, the site offers purchasing using PayPal.

Eric Zassenhaus, City Lights' "web guy" had this to say about the process:

"We're trying to change the nature of the site right now. We're becoming more of a commercial venue, selling through the site. We're just dipping our feet into the water, which is why we went with PayPal to start. We didn't have the resources for another solution, and it can be incredibly expensive. We're going to take the transition slow, starting with this option and seeing how it goes."

1.8

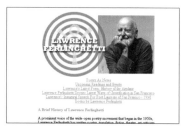

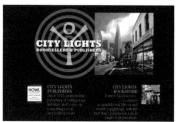

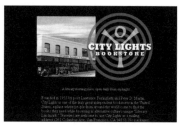

1.8 Screenshots from **CITYLIGHTS.COM**.

▶

With a strong understanding and plan for your website in place, you're ready to step through the creation of a small business site for promotions. This book is here to help you create a successful business site but is limited in its scope to teach you all the design and technology you'll need to implement the site.

To help with that issue, you'll be working from a design template that includes sample graphics and code you'll use to design your initial site. Using the tools provided, you can then customise the template to your needs. You'll use the work you do here later in the book, too, when you add special features of interest to the site.

But before jumping into working with the templates, you'll also want an understanding of what content and page types are necessary to include within a small business site for promotions. Using the example of the lawyer, I'll step you through defining your site areas, gathering the necessary items, and working with the site template components to create the site.

avabooks.ch/dyo/eshop

NOTE

Please see the book's web page at avabooks.ch/dyo/eshop for downloads and information.

◀◀

Pages You'll be Using

In order to get a sense of what's needed, I've revisited the mission statement for the lawyer's site, highlighting those concepts that relate directly to a unique page as follows:

" The intent of my site is to promote my legal services to the members of my local community. The site provides a **description of my services and specialty in the area of estate law**, information about **my education, background**, and **interests**, and **complete contact information** for potential clients to get in touch."

From the mission statement, I came up with the following outline of sections: Home Page (Welcome), About Estate Law, Services, About the Lawyer and Getting in Touch.

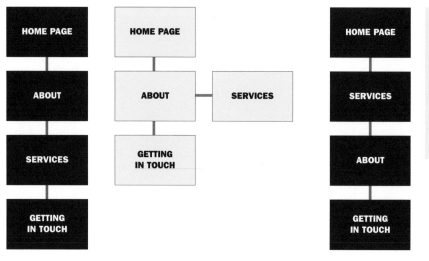

NOTE

Consider writing down individual keywords related to your mission statement on index cards. Then, move the cards around in different ways to figure out how your website might be organised.

The Home Page provides the welcome, with enough information about the site's intent to capture the audience's interest. The About Estate Law section helps provide visitors with a frequently asked questions (FAQ) page that explains in detail the lawyer's specialty. The Services page provides a listing of the type of services available, such as will planning, trusts, and so forth. About the Lawyer is a perfect place for a photo, curriculum vitae, and professional biography. Finally, the Getting in Touch page offers the phone, FAX, and any other relevant numbers and the location including driving directions and a map, making access to the lawyer's office easy.

For a small site like this one – which is promoting a company rather than featuring specific products – about five pages is more than enough. Go ahead and examine your site needs, and organise the pages you'd like to have into a list just as I have.

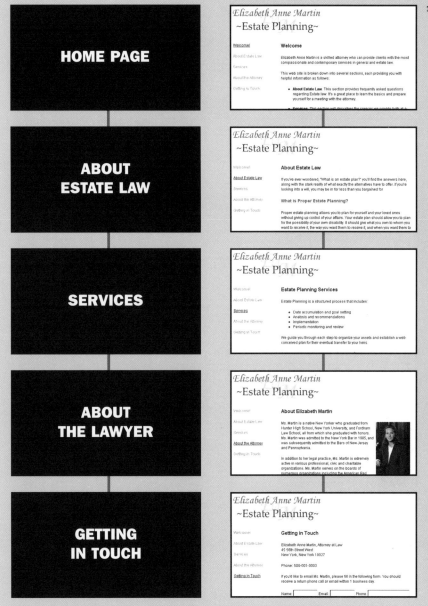

1.9 The five main sections of the lawyer's site include the following: home page, about estate law, services, about the lawyer and getting in touch.

Creating the Website

1.10

Elizabeth Anne Martin
~Estate Planning~

Welcome!

About Estate Law

Services

About the Attorney

Getting in Touch

Welcome

Elizabeth Anne Martin is a skilled attorney who can provide clients with the most compassionate and contemporary services in general and estate law.

This web site is broken down into several sections, each providing you with helpful information as follows:

- **About Estate Law**. This section provides frequently asked questions regarding Estate law. It's a great place to learn the basics and prepare yourself for a meeting with the attorney.

- **Services**. This section will describes the services we provide both at-a-glance and in greater detail.

- **About the Attorney**. Get to know Ms. Martin, who has served her Estate clients for over 20 years with professionalism and great attention to detail.

- **Getting in Touch**. Complete contact information, driving instructions, and a map to get you to your appointment on time!

Please enjoy the site, and should you have any questions or concerns about the site or the services described herein, please contact the site administrator ean@blahblah.com.

Now you'll step through the process of working with the website template used for this sample. The first thing to do is download the site components, available from the book's web page at **avabooks.ch/dyo/eshop**.

Once you've got the files in hand, you'll want to get familiar with them. Some ways of doing this include:

- **Open the file named legal-index.html in your web browser.**

- **Explore the pages using the links within the document.**

- **Select View > Source from your browser menu to take a look at the code the template uses.**

- **Open the pages in your editor. This can be NotePad on Windows, or SimpleText on Macintosh computers. You'll make all changes and edits to your pages here.**

Once you're familiar with the documents, the idea is to fashion your own site using the templates provided as a guideline.

1.10 Here's the original template file as it appears in Internet Explorer.

DYO E-Shop Toolbox:

▶

Things You'll Need

An editor (Text or HTML)

You can use the free editors that come with your operating system (Notepad for Windows, SimpleText for Macintosh), download an editor from the web (try Homesite from Macromedia, macromedia.com), or buy a software package that helps you build websites such as Microsoft FrontPage (microsoft.com), Adobe GoLive (adobe.com), or Macromedia Dreamweaver (macromedia.com).

An image editor

You can use a shareware editor such as Paint Shop Pro (jasc.com), or purchase a higher-end image editor such as Photoshop (adobe.com) if you are planning to do a lot of graphic images for your site, such as might be required of an online store.

An FTP client

This is the software that allows you to move your finished documents to your web server. For more on server solutions, please see Chapter 2.

Creating the Logo

If you open file legal-logo.gif in your image editing software, you'll notice that the image is 350 pixels wide by 100 pixels high and contains text.

1.11

300

100

You can create your own logo by following these steps:

In your image editor, select File > New.

The New dialog will open. It will be different depending upon the imaging program, but most are very similar in their navigation so you should have no problem following along. Create a new file that is 300 pixels wide by 100 pixels in height.

Using the Text tool in your program, create a logo appropriate for your site. You may also add shapes, objects, or any existing logographic designs.

Save your graphic file in a suitable web format (GIF or JPEG). See your image editing program for more documentation on how to save for the web should it not be an obvious option within your editor. You can name the file as you see fit, it will replace the legal-logo.gif file in the source code.

1.11 Shown here is the logo for the lawyer's website and its size in pixels.

Adding the Logo to the Page

Once you've created the logo, the next step is to add it to the page. To do so, follow these steps:

Open the legal-index.html file in your editing program. Be sure you are in an actual editor and can type in changes.

Find this section of code, located toward the top of the file:

```
<!— replace legal-logo.gif in the source below with your logo
file's name —>

<div id="Layer1" style="position:absolute; left:8px;
top:10px; width:300px; height:100px; z-index:1"><img
src="legal-logo.gif" width="300" height="100"></div>
```

Replace the highlighted name with your file's name.

Save the file as index.html.

You should now view the file in your web browser, and see the new logo you created is now integrated into the page.

Modifying the Links

If you followed the steps outlined earlier in the chapter, you should by now have a list of site sections you'll need for your specific site. Since they'll likely be different than the ones here, you'll want to modify them as required.

Consider the following code:

```
<p><a href="index.html">Welcome!</a></p>
<p><a href="estate.html">About Estate Law</a></p>
<p><a href="services.html">Services</a></p>
<p><a href="about.html">About the Attorney</a></p>
<p><a href="contact.html">Getting in Touch</a></p>
```

Each of these lines creates the link content and the link itself. You can see I've named my files simply: "about.html" and "contact.html" are very clear file names. You should try to do the same, keeping your file names short. The same is true of the link content names themselves, such as "About the Attorney".

NOTE

You'll need to make sure the links you created are consistent on every page you create.

1.12

In your editor, rename the link file names and content names as you see fit. So, if your file contains a list of books you're selling, you'll swap:

```
<p><a href="estate.html">About Estate Law</a></p>
```

For something akin to:

```
<p><a href="booklist.html">Current Book List</a></p>
```

Change as many links as you require, and be sure not to forget to change the mail link at the bottom of the page, too. Simply replace your correct email address in the file and content section of the link. When you're finished, save your file.

1.12 Storefront examples above and opposite include **MACKINTOSHDESIGN.COM**, **MONNETTELEATHERDESIGN.COM** and **DRYMARTINI.COM**.

▸▸

◀◀

Adding and Modifying Content

At this point, the goal is to customise the content itself. Using the index.html page you've just created, create a site template by saving the page again as template.html. Now, each time you want to create a new page, you'll open this template, rename the file as needed, and add your content.

To add header and paragraph text:

Simply highlight any existing text that you do not want and type in the new content appropriate for your site.

To add images:

You can add any images you have by manually entering the code for the image:

```
<img src="x" width="x" height="x" alt="x">
```

1.13

1.13

1.14

Image Size

Pixel Dimensions: 50K (was 61K)

Width: 168 pixels

Height: 100 pixels

Document Size:

Width: 5.94 cm

Height: 3.53 cm

Resolution: 72 pixels/inch

☑ Constrain Proportions
☑ Resample Image: Bicubic

OK
Cancel
Auto…

You'll need to fill in the values of x as follows:

src="x" – replace x with your image name and file extension, such as sculpture1.jpg.

width="x" – replace x with your image's width in pixels (you can find this in your imaging program under image size).

height="x" – replace x with your image's height in pixels (also found in your imaging program).

alt="x" – provide a short but descriptive sentence about the image, such as "sculpture of female form in bronze". Alt attribute descriptions assist those people with vision problems or blindness to gain a better understanding of what the images on the page represent.

1.13 Girlshop and Guyshop use whimsical and offbeat imagery to present their content, **GIRLSHOP.COM**, **GUYSHOP.COM**. If you visit these sites you will see that the characters are animated slightly: the guy taps his foot while the girl swings her handbag.

1.14 The Image Size interface in Adobe Photoshop.

Changing Colours & Fonts

If you don't like the colours and fonts for the template, you can make changes in the style sheet file. This is the file that ends in .css. Open up the file in your editor and consider the following code:

```css
body {
        font-family: Arial, Helvetica, sans-serif;
        font-size: 16px;
        line-height: 22px;
        color: #660000;
        background-color: #FFFFFF;
}
a:link {
        font-family: Arial, Helvetica, sans-serif;
        font-size: 16px;
        color: #666633;
        text-decoration: none;
}
a:visited {
        font-family: Arial, Helvetica, sans-serif;
        font-size: 16px;
        color: #999933;
        text-decoration: none;
}
a:active {
        font-family: Arial, Helvetica, sans-serif;
        font-size: 16px;
        color: #996633;
        text-decoration: none;
}
a:hover {
        font-family: Arial, Helvetica, sans-serif;
        font-size: 16px;
        color: #660000;
        text-decoration: underline;
}
```

To change colours, simply find the hexadecimal equivalent of the colour you'd like for each feature described in the style sheet, and replace it.

000000	003300	006600	009900	00CC00	00FF00
000033	003333	006633	009933	00CC33	00FF33
000066	003366	006666	009966	00CC66	00FF66
000099	003399	006699	009999	00CC99	00FF99
0000CC	0033CC	0066CC	0099CC	00CCCC	00FFCC
0000FF	0033FF	0066FF	0099FF	00CCFF	00FFFF
330000	333300	336600	339900	33CC00	33FF00
330033	333333	336633	339933	33CC33	33FF33
330066	333366	336666	339966	33CC66	33FF66
330099	333399	336699	339999	33CC99	33FF99
3300CC	3333CC	3366CC	3399CC	33CCCC	33FFCC
3300FF	3333FF	3366FF	3399FF	33CCFF	33FFFF
660000	663300	666600	669900	66CC00	66FF00
660033	663333	666633	669933	66CC33	66FF33
660066	663366	666666	669966	66CC66	66FF66
660099	663399	666699	669999	66CC99	66FF99
6600CC	6633CC	6666CC	6699CC	66CCCC	66FFCC
6600FF	6633FF	6666FF	6699FF	66CCFF	66FFFF
990000	993300	996600	999900	99CC00	99FF00
990033	993333	996633	999933	99CC33	99FF33
990066	993366	996666	999966	99CC66	99FF66
990099	993399	996699	999999	99CC99	99FF99
9900CC	9933CC	9966CC	9999CC	99CCCC	99FFCC
9900FF	9933FF	9966FF	9999FF	99CCFF	99FFFF
CC0000	CC3300	CC6600	CC9900	CCCC00	CCFF00
CC0033	CC3333	CC6633	CC9933	CCCC33	CCFF33
CC0066	CC3366	CC6666	CC9966	CCCC66	CCFF66
CC0099	CC3399	CC6699	CC9999	CCCC99	CCFF99
CC00CC	CC33CC	CC66CC	CC99CC	CCCCCC	CCFFCC
CC00FF	CC33FF	CC66FF	CC99FF	CCCCFF	CCFFFF
FF0000	FF3300	FF6600	FF9900	FFCC00	FFFF00
FF0033	FF3333	FF6633	FF9933	FFCC33	FFFF33
FF0066	FF3366	FF6666	FF9966	FFCC66	FFFF66
FF0099	FF3399	FF6699	FF9999	FFCC99	FFFF99
FF00CC	FF33CC	FF66CC	FF99CC	FFCCCC	FFFFCC
FF00FF	FF33FF	FF66FF	FF99FF	FFCCFF	FFFFFF

1.15 The above hexadecimal chart can be found at **MOLLY.COM/MOLLY/WEBDESIGN/COLORCHART.HTML**.

◄◄

Under any instance of font-family, you may change the fonts to your taste. Be forewarned, however, that the fonts you choose may not be available on everyone's machines. That's why it's best to stick to common fonts and font combinations. Some safe combinations you might like to try and include:

Times New Roman, Times, serif
Courier New, Courier, mono
Georgia, Times New Roman, Times, serif
Verdana, Arial, Helvetica, sans-serif
Geneva, Arial, Helvetica, sans-serif

Make the changes to the style sheet using your editor, and then save the file. View your page in your web browser to see the updated changes. When you're ready, use your FTP client or other software provided by your Internet Service Provider to upload your site to the web.

Serif

abcdefghijklmnopqrstuvwxyz 1234567890 ABCDEFGHIJKLMNOPQRSTUVWXYZ
Times New Roman
abcdefghijklmnopqrstuvwxyz 1234567890 ABCDEFGHIJKLMNOPQRSTUVWXYZ
Georgia

Mono

abcdefghijklmnopqrstuvwxyz 1234567890 ABCDEFGHIJKLMNOPQRSTUVWXYZ
Courier New
abcdefghijklmnopqrstuvwxyz 1234567890 ABCDEFGHIJKLMNOPQRSTUVWXYZ
Courier

Sans-serif

abcdefghijklmnopqrstuvwxyz 1234567890 ABCDEFGHIJKLMNOPQRSTUVWXYZ
Verdana
abcdefghijklmnopqrstuvwxyz 1234567890 ABCDEFGHIJKLMNOPQRSTUVWXYZ
Arial
abcdefghijklmnopqrstuvwxyz 1234567890 ABCDEFGHILKJMNOPQRSTUVWXYZ
Helvetica
abcdefghijklmnopqrstuvwxyz 1234567890 ABCDEFGHIJKLMNOPQRSTUVWXYZ
Geneva

1.16

Arial

Courier   Helvetica

Verdana

1.16 The fonts you choose can affect the layout as some fonts occupy more space than others, as shown above.

Coming up next:

In just one chapter you've created a simple site that very cleanly and effectively promotes a small business. In the next chapter, you'll learn about merchant accounts, which are a necessary means of allowing purchasing on your website.

SETTING UP MERCHANT ACCOUNTS

▶

In order to allow purchasing on your website, you must have some way of enabling your site visitors to pay the charges, fees, taxes, shipping, and any other costs that might be incurred at your site.

Prior to the web, the term merchant account referred exclusively to an account that a merchant would set up with his or her bank to accept credit cards. These accounts still exist today of course, you use them regularly wherever you might use your credit card: a restaurant, a hair salon, a specialty food shop, or when you order something from a catalogue.

In the early days of the web, there were only a few ways to accept payments online, and pretty clumsy ones at that. The main choice in those days was to set up a merchant account, but with far fewer options than those available now. At that time, getting a merchant account meant going to your bank, filling out lots of forms, having your credit checked, paying certain fees, getting the equipment necessary to run credit cards, and so forth. Before the advent of e-commerce and secure transactions, however, this still meant having to have the site visitor call, FAX, or worse yet in terms of security, send his or her credit card information in email or over an insecure web-based form.

WHILE YOU MAY ONLY BE INTERESTED IN HAVING A PROMOTIONAL WEBSITE SUCH AS THE ONE YOU JUST BUILT IN CHAPTER 1, MANY READERS OF THIS BOOK WILL WANT TO SELL THEIR GOODS AND SERVICES DIRECTLY ONLINE.

◀◀

Other means of accepting payments for online services were more conventional: Accepting cheques or money orders for example, which customers would have to mail via standard postal services prior to the item being shipped. As you can see, this made electronic shopping a rather limited venture, especially when one considers that then, as now, the web is an international forum. So, payments would have to be corrected for local currency exchange rates. Also, cheques from another country can take longer to process, meaning the customer is waiting a very long time before their product or service can be delivered.

But with the arrival and proliferation of e-commerce and its related security and technical speed, the merchant account has changed a great deal, and there is now a range of merchant accounts to choose from. Such accounts include:

Standard merchant account

This is the same old-fashioned type of account, where you as the merchant must contact a bank, fill out a range of forms, have credit checks run, and pay bank and other fees related to merchant accounts. But nowadays, instead of having to manually run such charges, these charges can be automated and kept secure with Internet payment services. Merchant accounts are sometimes limited in various ways. For example, you might be able to take credit cards only, rather than credit and debit cards.

Alternative online payment options

Several companies offer alternatives to standard or online merchant accounts, allowing purchasers to use cash, cheques, credit, or debit cards to start an account with that company (not you) and then pay you from the money available in their specialty account. The most notable service of this kind is PayPal, and its tremendous success integration into eBay shows just how important a role that alternative options can play in e-commerce, at both small and large scale.

Managed online merchant accounts

If you're looking for a broader solution where you can accept credit cards, debit cards, even personal cheques, a range of merchant accounts with an emphasis on flexibility, security, and internationalised payment options is available. Some of these are solutions you buy and then implement, while others are customised and managed according to your needs by an online service provider.

2.1

2.1 Many successful sites, including eBay (**EBAY.CO.UK**), use PayPal (**PAYPAL.COM**) as an alternative online payment service.

Paying the Bill

▶

Just as your customers will be paying you, you have to pay for merchant account services – there simply is no way around this fact – not if you want to be able to accept credit cards directly!

Rates and fees range in great detail depending upon a number of factors, including:

- The kind of goods and services you're offering

- The volume of sales you conduct

- Your credit rating

- Length of time in business

- The method of merchant service you choose

Common fees of which to be aware include:

- Security deposits

- Initial set-up fees

- Necessary software purchase and installation (this is limited to those solutions you provide on your own server)

- Monthly service charges

- Per-transaction fees

- Fraud protection fees

Not all these fees will be required – it largely depends upon the service you manage to find.

2.2 Sample purchasing screens from **CHERRYGAL.COM**, **FIRECOLLECTIBLES.COM** and **BUFFALOEXCHANGE.COM**.

So if you're interested in effectively offering your site visitors options as to how they might purchase your goods with flexibility, security, and ease, you'll want to know more about these individual types of merchant accounts, what you'll need to get started, and what setting up various account types entails.

2.2

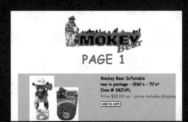

▶

If you are taking an existing business to the web, a standard merchant account with your bank combined with some Design Your Own savvy can make installing credit transaction capabilities on your website fairly straightforward.

The first step is getting approved, which may not always be easy. Standard merchant accounts tend to be a bit challenging to obtain because banks are, understandably, highly selective when it comes to providing services that contain inherent risks such as fraud or non-payment of required fees.

The criteria banks look for before providing a client with a merchant account is generally as follows:

- You have been in business for at least two years

- You have an established relationship with the bank

- You have a good or excellent credit history

- You have an idea of your average order size per month

- You have an idea of your average revenue per month

- You know the credit cards you'd like to accept
  (MasterCard and Visa are typically lower-cost than American Express, for example)

Of course, depending upon which bank you speak with, other criteria may be of concern. Talk to your banker. Most major banks worldwide are familiar with the specific needs of merchant accounts for online buyers.

With Account in Hand...

Once you have acquired your merchant account from the bank, you'll have to be prepared to acquire and implement a number of items including:

– Ensuring your Internet Service Provider (ISP) has security technology such as SSL available to you

– Choosing an Internet payment processing system (if your ISP doesn't have one available)

– Building a form or adding a link to your site to facilitate payment via the processing system

NOTE

Using a simple purchase form is best for the small merchant with single or few items on offer. Be sure to read about *Shopping Cart Solutions* in Chapter 3, which shows more complex options for multiple purchases.

STEP 1:
ACQUIRE SECURE SERVICE FROM YOUR ISP

If you already have a hosting service for your website, you'll want to talk to them about secure transactions. Most, but not all, ISPs offer this kind of service, and of course it will have a fee attached to it. You've really got to do some of your own research to find the best balance of cost and service quality.

Choosing an ISP isn't an easy issue. So much will depend upon how you want to run your site. As you'll read later on in this chapter, there are ISPs that offer highly managed services. You can view a list of providers in the Resource section later in this book, too.

Your ISP's geographical location is not a matter of concern. Rather, focus on whether the provider is reliable and available to professionally serve your needs. Many companies

successfully purchase service provision in multiple locations around the world, depending upon their website delivery needs.

For secure transactions, you're especially looking for an ISP that offers Secure Sockets Layer (SSL). This is a widely-used and trusted security and encryption method by which sensitive data such as credit card numbers can be safely transmitted, and also provides a digital certificate identifying where the data is coming from, making access to sensitive data even more difficult. Many ISPs will provide both the SSL and the related Internet payment processing system, so all you have to worry about is creating the purchasing form.

2.4

NOTE

For general information on finding service providers, see thelist.com.

2.4 Sample ISPs found from a simple search on **THELIST.COM**, and opposite, a listing from the website.

A + Net
ISDN, 33.6, 28.8, 56K
T3, Frame Relay, FracT3, T1

A 007 Access
ISDN, 33.6, 28.8, 56K
T3, Frame Relay, FracT3, T1, DSL

A 1 A 1Monster
ISDN, 33.6, 28.8, 56K

A 1 Excel Internet
33.6, 28.8, 56K

A Access 750
33.6, 28.8, 56K

AA-mail.net
ISDN, 33.6, 28.8, 56K
Frame Relay, DSL

Aarisnet Internet
ISDN, 33.6, 28.8, 56K

Absolute Web Access.net
33.6, 28.8, 56K

777Access
56K

550 Access
33.6, 28.8, 56K

Access Kentucky
ISDN, 33.6, 28.8, 56K, T1, DSL

Acer Access
ISDN, 33.6, 28.8, 56K

Admiral Online
33.6, 28.8, 56K, T3, Frame Relay,
FracT3, T1, DSL

Advanced-Connect.Net
56K
T1, DSL

Airewaves Broadband, LLC
56K
T3, Frame Relay, FracT3, T1

Alacrity Internet
ISDN, 33.6, 28.8, 56K

alfnet.net, Inc.
ISDN, 56K
Frame Relay, T1, DSL
33.6, 28.8, 56K

Ameralinx
ISDN, 33.6, 28.8, 56K
T1, DSL

Ameranet.Com
33.6, 28.8, 56K

American Digital Networks
ISDN, 33.6, 28.8, 56K
T3, Frame Relay, FracT3, T1, DSL

Americas Internet. Net
ISDN, 56K
DSL

Americasisp.us
33.6, 28.8, 56K

Anglin Internet Service
ISDN, 33.6, 28.8, 56K

aPerfectHost
33.6, 28.8, 56K
ISDN, 33.6, 28.8, 56K
DSL

ArchitecturalWorld
33.6, 28.8, 56K

AreaTech
ISDN, 56K

Arrowheadnet.com
33.6, 28.8, 56K
FracT3, DSL

ASAP WorldNET
ISDN, 33.6, 28.8, 56K

At The World
33.6, 28.8, 56K
T3, Frame Relay, FracT3, T1, DSL
56K, DSL

AtYourNET Connection
ISDN, 33.6, 28.8, 56K
T3, Frame Relay, FracT3, T1

Aztecnet.net
ISDN, 33.6, 28.8, 56K

AZWEST INTERNET SERVICES INC
ISDN, 33.6, 28.8, 56K

B on the Web
ISDN, 56K
T3, Frame Relay, FracT3, T1, DSL

bargainisp.net
33.6, 28.8, 56K
T3, Frame Relay, FracT3, T1, DSL

Bbe Computers Internet Service
56K, DSL

Big Dog ISP
ISDN, 56K

BlueHome.Net
33.6, 28.8, 56K

BlueLight
33.6, 28.8, 56K

Broadbandez
Dsl, 56K
T3, FracT3, T1, DSL

Budget Dialup, Inc.
33.6, 28.8, 56K

Budgetspeed.Com
ISDN, 33.6, 28.8, 56K

Budgetsurf Network
ISDN, 33.6, 28.8, 56K

Buzell
ISDN, 33.6, 28.8, 56K

Buzell.com Internet Services
ISDN, 33.6, 28.8, 56K

C & K Marketing
33.6, 28.8, 56K

C&D Enterprizes Ltd.
ISDN, 33.6, 28.8, 56K
T3, Frame Relay, FracT3, T1

C3 Online Internet Services
ISDN, 33.6, 28.8, 56K

Cable & Wireless
56K T3, Frame Relay, FracT3, T1, DSL

CAL-TEK
56K

Catholic Internet Services Inc
ISDN, 33.6, 28.8, 56K

Cheap
56k, ISDN, 33.6, 28.8, 56K

Cisp
ISDN, 33.6, 28.8, 56K
T3, Frame Relay, FracT3, T1, DSL

Clearshot Communications LLC
ISDN, 33.6, 28.8, 56K

Cleartouch.Com
ISDN, 56K
T3, Frame Relay, FracT3, T1, DSL

Clockwatchers, Inc.
56K

ClubDepot
33.6, 28.8, 56K

Conceptscorp
56K

Config.com, Inc.
ISDN, 33.6, 28.8, 56K
T1

Connect Internet Services, Inc
ISDN, 33.6, 28.8, 56K
Frame Relay, DSL

CPU-NET.COM, INC
ISDN, 33.6, 28.8, 56K

Creative Internet USA
33.6, 28.8, 56K
DSL

Cros.net, Inc.
ISDN, 33.6, 28.8, 56K
T3, Frame Relay, FracT3, T1, DSL

Crystal Clear P.C.
56K
Frame Relay, T1

Crystal Mountain BBS
ISDN, 33.6, 28.8, 56K

Cwic, Ltd.
ISDN, 33.6, 28.8, 56K

cyberM.I.N.D.
ISDN, 33.6, 28.8, 56K
T3, Frame Relay, FracT3, T1, DSL

3D Internet
ISDN, 33.6, 28.8, 56K

Dallas Net
ISDN, 33.6, 56K
T3, Frame Relay

Data Dave'S Computer Solutions
33.6, 28.8, 56K

Data Packet Networks
ISDN, 33.6, 28.8, 56K
FracT3, T1

Delmarva Net Internet Services
ISDN, 33.6, 28.8, 56K

deluxeHOST.com
ISDN, 33.6, 28.8, 56K
Frame Relay, T1, DSL

deluxehost.com
ISDN, 56K
Frame Relay, T1

Design House Technologies Inc
ISDN, 33.6, 28.8, 56K
T3, Frame Relay, FracT3, T1

Design Plateau Internet Services, Inc.
ISDN, 56K

Dexo.Net
56K

DGUI
56K

Dialup Usa, Inc.
ISDN, 33.6, 28.8, 56K
DSL

Dialup-Accounts.Com
ISDN, 33.6, 28.8, 56K

1095dialup.com
ISDN, 33.6, 28.8, 56K
T1, DSL

Digital Caffeine
ISDN, 33.6, 28.8, 56K

DS-iSolutions, Inc
ISDN, 56K

Dsl.Com Inc.
DSL

Dt Click
ISDN, 33.6, 28.8, 56K
Frame Relay, T1

E20n
33.6, 28.8, 56K
T3, Frame Relay, FracT3, T1, DSL
ISDN, 33.6, 28.8, 56K

ECS
ISDN, 33.6, 28.8, 56K
T3, Frame Relay, FracT3, T1, DSL

edconnect.net
ISDN, 33.6, 28.8, 56K

Edconnect.net
33.6, 28.8, 56K

Emailit.Com
33.6, 28.8, 56K
DSL

Enspirion, Inc.
56K
DSL

Eriex
ISDN, 33.6, 28.8, 56K
DSL

Eskimo North, Inc.
ISDN, 33.6, 28.8, 56K
Frame Relay, T1

Ets Communications
ISDN, 33.6, 28.8, 56K
T3, Frame Relay, FracT3, T1, DSL

Excel
56K

Excel Communications
28.8, 56K

Fast Dependable Access
33.6, 28.8, 56K
T1

123 Flash.net
ISDN, 33.6, 28.8, 56K

Gamefreek.net
ISDN, 33.6, 28.8, 56K
T3, Frame Relay, FracT3, T1, DSL

GenisysHosting Services
33.6, 28.8, 56K

Get Wired El Paso
ISDN, 33.6, 28.8, 56K

Globalaccess1.Com
ISDN, 56K

Globalband Networks
ISDN, 33.6, 28.8, 56K

GlobalNet
ISDN, 33.6, 28.8, 56K
T3, Frame Relay, FracT3, T1, DSL

GlobalNet-USA.net
56K
T3, Frame Relay, FracT3, T1, DSL

21Globe, Inc.
33.6, 28.8, 56K
T3, Frame Relay, FracT3, T1, DSL

GoldSurf.net
33.6, 28.8, 56K

Haignet
56K

Heypete.Com
ISDN, 33.6, 28.8, 56K

Host Monterey.com
56K
DSL

HostNed ISP
33.6, 28.8, 56K

Hyperconnections, Inc.
ISDN, 33.6, 28.8, 56K

I 5 Network Solutions
33.6, 28.8, 56K
DSL

I70West Online Services
ISDN, 33.6, 28.8, 56K

Idial.Net
33.6, 28.8, 56K
T3, Frame Relay, FracT3, T1, DSL

Inercom Communications Inc.
ISDN, 33.6, 28.8, 56K
T3, FracT3, T1, DSL

995 INET
ISDN, 33.6, 28.8, 56K

Inter-Akt.Com Llc
ISDN, 33.6, 28.8, 56K

Intercom Online Inc.
56K
T3, Frame Relay, FracT3, T1

@iNTERLYNC.com
ISDN, 33.6, 28.8, 56K
DSL

Internet Central
ISDN, 33.6, 28.8, 56K
T3, Frame Relay, FracT3, T1, DSL

Internet Connection
ISDN, 56K
T3, Frame Relay, FracT3, T1, DSL

Internet Services And Communic
ISDN, 33.6, 28.8, 56K
T3, Frame Relay, FracT3, T1, DSL

Internetwork Solutions
ISDN, 33.6, 28.8, 56K

IP Access America
33.6, 28.8, 56K
T3, Frame Relay, FracT3, T1

Iphostway.com
ISDN, 33.6, 28.8, 56K
FracT3, T1, DSL

ISeePower.Net
ISDN, 33.6, 28.8, 56K
Frame Relay, T1

ISP America
33.6, 28.8, 56K
T3, Frame Relay, FracT3, T1, DSL

ISP Unlimited
56K
DSL

ISP West
ISDN, 33.6, 28.8, 56K

ISP-SOLUTION
ISDN, 33.6, 28.8, 56K

4ISP.Net / TangiNet
ISDN, 33.6, 28.8, 56K

ispEZ
T1

ISPKC
ISDN, 33.6, 28.8, 56K

ISPpc.com
56K

ISPSaver
56K

Joe Galaxy, LLC
ISDN, 33.6, 28.8, 56K
T3, FracT3, T1, DSL

Karma Technologies LLC
ISDN, 33.6, 28.8, 56K
T3, FracT3, T1, DSL

Kingdom Online
33.6, 28.8, 56K

KwikIT.com - eMallsAmerica, Inc.
56K

LightNet
ISDN, 33.6, 28.8, 56K
DSL

1+ Long Distance Network
ISDN, 33.6, 28.8, 56K
T1

lovedialup
33.6, 28.8, 56K

Macrevolution
ISDN, 33.6, 28.8, 56K
T1

macrunner
33.6, 28.8, 56K
T1

Mad River Access
ISDN, 33.6, 28.8, 56K

Map Services
ISDN, 33.6, 28.8, 56K
DSL

Marathon Computers
56K
T3, Frame Relay, FracT3, T1, DSL

Markosoftplus
ISDN, 33.6, 28.8, 56K

Mcriders.Com
33.6, 28.8, 56K
DSL

MegaPlanet Internet Services
33.6, 28.8, 56K

mFire
56K

Microthought Network
ISDN, 33.6, 28.8, 56K
T3, FracT3, T1, DSL

Mindspring
33.6, 28.8, 56K
DSL

MM2K
ISDN, 33.6, 28.8, 56K
T3, Frame Relay, FracT3, T1, DSL

MOI Online
ISDN, 33.6, 28.8, 56K
Frame Relay, T1

Morethanisp
33.6, 28.8, 56K
DSL,

Mundonuevo.Com, Inc.
ISDN, 33.6, 28.8, 56K
T3, Frame Relay, FracT3, T1

My Web Star
33.6, 28.8, 56K

My56k
33.6, 28.8, 56K

MyExcel Internet
ISDN, 33.6, 28.8, 56K

MyMinimum
ISDN, 56K

MySDFS
56K

MyTag
33.6, 28.8, 56K

Nanomega.Com
ISDN, 33.6, 28.8, 56K
T3, Frame Relay, FracT3, T1, DSL

Napu.Net Div. Of Lou. Telecom
ISDN, 33.6, 28.8, 56K

nascarfan
ISDN, 33.6, 28.8, 56K

NCCW Online Inc.
33.6, 28.8, 56K

Ncol.Net
Frame Relay, T1, DSL

711.Net
33.6, 28.8, 56K

NetAccess, Inc
ISDN, 56K
T3, Frame Relay, FracT3, T1, DSL

NetHost
33.6, 28.8, 56K

NetValve USA, Inc.
ISDN, 33.6, 28.8, 56K

Netvero
ISDN, 33.6, 28.8, 56K

New Jersey Computer Connection
ISDN, 33.6, 28.8, 56K
Frame Relay, T1, DSL

Nswe Corporation
33.6, 28.8, 56K

Nu-World Communications
56K
Frame Relay, T1, DSL

Nubonyx.Com
33.6, 28.8, 56K

Office Keeper ISP
56K

Okpride.Net Llc
33.6, 28.8, 56K

OnlineTX Internet Service
33.6, 28.8, 56K

Osnet
ISDN, 33.6, 28.8, 56K
DSL

PC WEB TECH
56K

Pcstarnet Services
33.6, 28.8, 56K
DSL

Pds2k.Com
T3, Frame Relay, FracT3, T1

Phreego, LLC.
56K
T3, Frame Relay, FracT3, T1, DSL

Platinum Web Services, Inc.
ISDN, 56K

PPSHOST.COM
56K

PremoWeb Internet Store
ISDN, 33.6, 28.8, 56K

Primeone Internet & Comm., Svc
33.6, 28.8, 56K

Prismlink.Net
ISDN, 33.6, 28.8, 56K

Private Pathways
ISDN, 33.6, 28.8, 56K

Racing Seat
ISDN, 33.6, 28.8, 56K

Rahis
ISDN, 33.6, 28.8, 56K

Rapidtower, Inc.
ISDN, 33.6, 28.8, 56K

Rdp Net
56K

Reynet.Com
ISDN, 33.6, 28.8, 56K
T1, DSL

Rocket Internet
ISDN, 56K

Rocketjet ISP
56K
T1

Route66isp.Com
33.6, 28.8, 56K

RPCom
ISDN, 33.6, 28.8, 56K

SafeRoam
33.6, 28.8, 56K

Sarver'S Output Services
33.6, 28.8, 56K
T1, DSL

Silicon Networks
33.6, 28.8, 56K
T3, FracT3, T1, DSL

SixFifty Internet
56K

Slpworld.net
33.6, 28.8, 56K

SMS Computer Services
ISDN, 33.6, 28.8, 56K
T3, FracT3, T1, DSL

SMS Dialup
ISDN, 33.6, 28.8, 56K
T3, Frame Relay, FracT3, T1, DSL

SolarData
ISDN, 33.6, 28.8, 56K
T3, Frame Relay, FracT3, T1, DSL

Southwest-Technology.Net
ISDN, 33.6, 28.8, 56K
DSL

Speakeasy.Net
56K
T1, DSL

Spearnet.Net
33.6, 28.8, 56K

Sprint
ISDN, 33.6, 28.8, 56K
T3, Frame Relay, FracT3, T1, DSL

1st.Net First Net
ISDN, 33.6, 28.8, 56K
T3, Frame Relay, FracT3, T1, DSL

Surf the Planet
ISDN, 56K

Surfcheap.Com (Wolftalk)
33.6, 28.8, 56K

Surferz.Net
ISDN, 33.6, 28.8, 56K
T3, Frame Relay, FracT3, T1, DSL

Sysmatrix.Net Nationwide Isp
33.6, 28.8, 56K

Sysnetex LLC
T3, T1, DSL

1 0 T O H O S T
ISDN, 33.6, 28.8, 56K
T3, Frame Relay, FracT3, T1

TCB Worldwide.NET
33.6, 28.8, 56K

TCQ Internet
33.6, 28.8, 56K
DSL

Tcw.Net
ISDN, 33.6, 28.8, 56K
T3, Frame Relay, FracT3, T1, DSL

TelBarato Internet
56K

Terapeta Corp
33.6, 28.8, 56K

Terrapath
T1, DSL

The World
ISDN, 33.6, 28.8, 56K

Tiger-Net
ISDN, 56K
T3, Frame Relay, FracT3, T1, DSL

1 To Surf The Net Now!
33.6, 28.8, 56K

TOAST.net
ISDN, 33.6, 56K
T3, Frame Relay, FracT3, T1, DSL

Triton Technologies
ISDN, 33.6, 28.8, 56K
T1, DSL

TRYSB.NET
ISDN, 33.6, 28.8, 56K
DSL

uGlide
56K

2uic.Net
ISDN, 33.6, 28.8, 56K
T1, DSL

UnixHosting
ISDN, 33.6, 28.8, 56K

UNUM Telecommunications, Inc.
ISDN, 33.6, 28.8, 56K
T3, Frame Relay, FracT3, T1

urastar2.net
ISDN, 33.6, 28.8, 56K
Frame Relay, FracT3, T1, DSL

US-ISP.NET
56K

Usbackbone
33.6, 28.8, 56K

USOL
56K

Value Internet Service
33.6, 28.8, 56K

VPM Internet Services, Inc.
56K
T3, Frame Relay, FracT3, T1, DSL

Walters & Associates
56K

Web Display Hosting Service
56K
FracT3, DSL

Web Pros Network
ISDN, 33.6, 28.8, 56K
DSL

Webcom U.S. Communications
ISDN, 56K

WebPathway
33.6, 28.8, 56K

WebWorkz ISP
ISDN, 33.6, 28.8, 56K

Whosthere.net
33.6, 28.8, 56K

World123.Net, Inc.
ISDN, 33.6, 28.8, 56K
T3, Frame Relay, FracT3, T1, DSL

Worldnurse.net
33.6, 28.8, 56K

WorldWide Wood/R-internet
ISDN, 33.6, 28.8, 56K

Wownet, Inc.
ISDN, 33.6, 28.8, 56K
DSL

WWCinter.net
33.6, 28.8, 56K

XO Communications
56K
T3, FracT3, T1, DSL

Xpress Internet
33.6, 28.8, 56K

YERISP
ISDN, 33.6, 28.8, 56K

yourEyeSP.com L.L.C.
ISDN, 56K
DSL

33.6, 28.8, 56K
DSL

STEP 2:
OBTAINING AN INTERNET PAYMENT PROCESSING SYSTEM

An Internet payment processing system provides the gateway that routes a customer's payment request to the proper financial institutions to authorise and process the payment.

Most small and medium-sized businesses will do well to outsource this portion of the process if it is not available on your ISP.

Verisign (Verisign.com) is one such company that has long been involved with outsourcing security and e-commerce transactions worldwide, and offers a line of products that can assist you with not only the security aspects of e-commerce, but the payment processing as well.

Because of its popularity and accessibility, I'll use it as an example of how processing systems work in general. But again – be sure to check with your ISP to see if they already have a payment processing service in place, or have a recommended one that they prefer to use.

For the small business, processing up to but not more than 500 transactions per month, you can use Verisign's Payflow Link service. With this service, a secure form sits on Verisign's SSL encrypted servers, along with the necessary digital certificates.

2.5

2.6

NOTE

Please see verisign.com/products/payflow/pricing.html for recent setup and monthly fees and other product options for those businesses requiring more than 500 transactions per month.

STEP 3:
ADD THE LINK TO YOUR PURCHASE PAGE

Once you have ascertained where you'll get your Internet payment processing system service, you'll simply need to add a link to your website that brings people to the secure ordering form.

The link code is provided to you by your ISP or by your processing system service, such as Verisign. You'll manually add this code to the proper page on your site. Once active, when the customer is ready to make a purchase, he or she follows the link, which takes them to this secure order form. There, the customer submits the required payment information. The transaction is verified (usually in a matter of seconds). With Verisign, an email is then sent to you and to your customer confirming the order. The payment is then processed, and the funds are transferred to your merchant account.

2.7

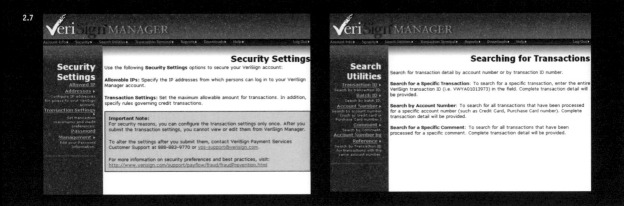

2.5 The Verisign logo.

2.6 Verisign is a leader in payment processing options for e-shop merchants.

2.7 Managing your payments online through Verisign's administration manager.

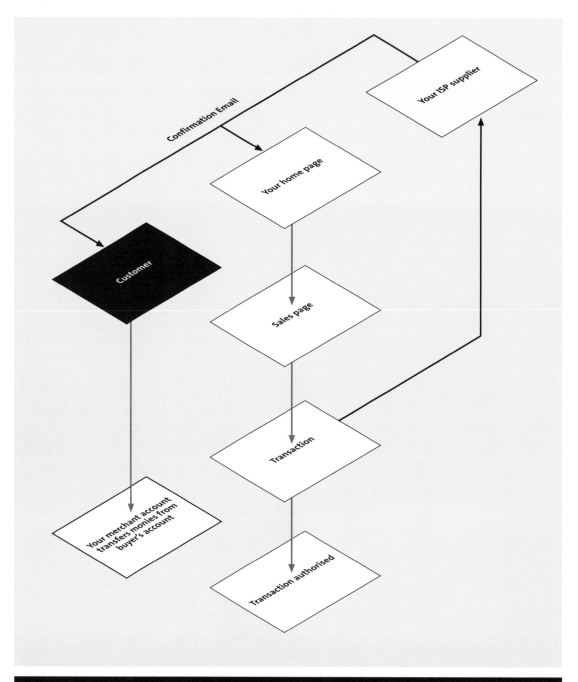

Your Merchant Account

Your merchant account enables customers to pay for their transactions using a credit card, making the online shopping experience highly convenient. Once all the web pages and backend technology is in place, a visitor to your site will find the product he or she would like and place the order. An email is then sent to the customer, providing confirmation of the order.

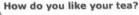

How do you like your tea?

HOT

16oz aria teapot
and three samples

only $15

ICED

32oz aria teapot
and tea pitcher

only $29

SEARCH: _____ GO

sugar shots
liquid cane sugar

stairway to bliss
organic tea - 1/3 off

tea / month club
free teapot

tea in a bottle
try the best

2.8 Screenshots from Adagio Teas, **ADAGIO.COM.**

The site was born with the idea of providing good tea to the 95% of the country whose brick-and-mortar options do not offer similar breadth or quality. It all began in a basement, with just one order on day one. The sole order came from my aunt," explains Michael Cramer, now Marketing Director of Adagio Teas.

Cramer is happy with the technologies he chose, saying that even during a busy Christmas in 2002, the site "held up pretty well". Cramer does go on to say that the merchant technologies and website at large are "now slated for a complete top-to-bottom redesign to allow for greater scalability in the future. And just

it card:

e on card:

l number:

Preventing Credit Card Fraud

As the merchant, you are liable for fraudulent transactions when the physical credit card is not available. If someone purchases a product from you using a fraudulent card and that person is caught, you won't recoup your money. So following these steps will help protect you from such losses.

There are several things you can do to protect yourself from fraud:

1 **Make sure your ISP and payment service providers are well known and have a good reputation.** Check online to see if anyone has submitted any complaints, or check with the business regulatory bureau in the city, state, and country where the companies in question do business.

2 **Choose real-time solutions.** Real-time processing solutions are considered safer because they authenticate the credit card number immediately. If the card has been lost, stolen, or is an invalid number, a real-time processing solution will not authorise the charge.

3 **Ask for credit card security codes on any input form.** There are special numbers on almost all credit cards that add an additional level of security. While this code isn't always used in processing the transaction, it can be an added security step. Asking for this code assists in verifying whether the owner of the card actually has the card in his or her possession.

4 **Watch for unusual purchasing habits, such as multiple orders of the same items.** This is especially true if the items you merchandise are items easily resold elsewhere (home electronics, cameras, and computer products, for example).

So, despite the high level of security offered for online transactions, nothing is perfect. Just as credit card fraud occurs in the real world so does it occur online, and you should follow these guidelines to preempt any potential problems.

ALTERNATIVE ONLINE PAYMENT OPTIONS

▶

If you're looking for the most hands-on way to accept payments online, alternative options may be the best solution for you. These options provide a variety of alternatives such as allowing both customers and merchants to exchange money online without directly inputting credit cards at the merchant site; access services that provide traditional billing methods to customers; and cash-based transaction services that enable people to make their online purchase by buying the virtual equivalent of a pre-paid phone card.

Some of the advantages of alternative online payment options include:

- Very low cost

- Scalability – it's a manageable solution for both small and large e-commerce businesses

- Flexibility – Alternative payment options allow people to make purchases based on their preferred method of payment: credit, debit, cheque – even cash

Because you are paying less, there can be some disadvantages:

- Instead of a seamless and familiar transaction process where the customer makes the purchase and then enters their credit card via a secure form, alternative processes vary in presentation. This can frustrate customers, many of whom want an easy-in, easy-out means of making online purchases.

NOTE

At the time of writing, PayPal was available in 37 countries. Note that there are certain transaction and service restrictions in some countries. Check paypal.com/cgi-bin/webscr?cmd=p/gen/approved_countries-outside for country and service details.

2.9 PayPal is considered the leader in alternative payment solutions.

The PayPal Model

PayPal, paypal.com, originally an independent alternative payment solution, became such an extremely popular way for merchants using eBay to make quick transactions that eBay bought the service. PayPal requires both the merchant and the buyer to have a PayPal account.

PayPal's basic service is available and free to any merchant and any buyer online who:

- Has an email address

- Has a credit card or

- Has a bank account

2.9

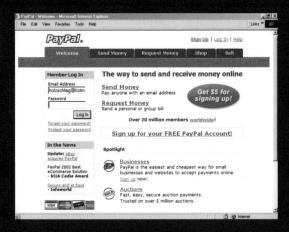

PayPal uses SSL technology, which makes it as secure as almost any other transaction service currently available. Also, you as the merchant will never see a customer's private information, only that the transaction has been completed. What's more, PayPal allows you to set the currency, and the exchange rate is managed automatically.

Setting Up a PayPal Account

In this section, you'll step through the process of setting up a standard PayPal account.

You will need a variety of information to hand, including:

- Personal identification and contact information
- Email address
- Security and password info

2.10 PayPal confirmation letter.

2.11 The PayPal interface.

To set up your account, follow these steps:

1 Point your browser to https://www.paypal.com/ cgi-bin/webscr?cmd=_registration-run.

2 Fill in the entire form properly and completely.

3 When finished, click Sign Up. PayPal will process your registration, and send a special link to your email address.

4 Go to your email and find the PayPal confirmation letter (Figure 2.10).

5 Click on the link that PayPal has provided. You'll be asked for your password, and then your email address will be confirmed as yours.

6 Click Continue. You will be taken directly to your account.

Once you're in the account interface (Figure 2.11) you'll be able to do a number of activities necessary to use PayPal both as a merchant. The first is to put the proper information on your website for purchases.

NOTE

You may set up an account in any available country. Here, I'll step you through the US model, as the process is the same for most other countries, too, and does not have certain restrictions as can be found in other countries. To set up an account outside of the United States, visit https://www.paypal.com/cgi-bin/webscr?cmd=international-register.

◀◀

The free account allows you to offer single item purchases only.
This means that each item will have a different item name, the currency
in which you'd like the transaction to be made, and the price of the
item. A different specialty link will be generated for each item, and
you then add that link on your web page to PayPal so anyone wanting
to purchase the item can do so.

2.12

2.12 Sample screenshots from **CHERRYGAL.COM**.

Here's the code that PayPal generated for an item on my website:

```
<form action="https://www.paypal.com/ cgi-
bin/webscr" method="post">

<input type="hidden" name="cmd" value="_xclick">

<input type="hidden" name="business"
value="holzschlag@hotmail.com">

<input type="hidden" name="item_name"
value="Design Your Own Homepage">

<input type="hidden" name="item_number"
value="DYO HP">

<input type="hidden" name="amount"
value="40.00">

<input type="hidden" name="no_note" value="1">

<input type="hidden" name="currency_code"
value="USD">

<input type="image"
src="https://www.paypal.com/images/x-click-
but23.gif" border="0" name="submit" alt="Make
payments with PayPal — it's fast, free and
secure!">

</form>
```

NOTE

PayPal offers very reasonably priced upgrade options to accounts wishing to create shopping carts and richer features for customers.
From your main account window, click "Upgrade" to learn more about the pay options available to you.

▶▶

In Figure 2.13, you can see how I added the code to my web page along with the PayPal "buy now" button. My site visitors can click on this button. They are then taken to the PayPal site, where they will either have an account or create a new one in order to make this, and other, PayPal purchases.

2.13

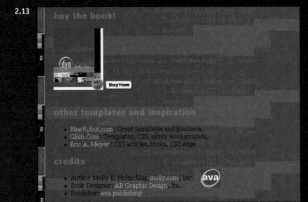

NOTE

Some e-shop merchants use both standard merchant accounts and PayPal to give their prospective customers more buying options.

2.13 Customers simply click PayPal's "Buy Now" button and are taken to PayPal to complete their purchase.

2.14 BABYUNIVERSE.COM provides a Bill Me Later payment option.

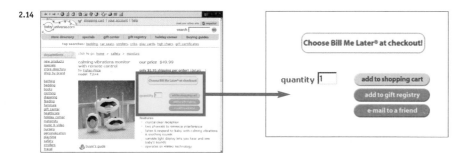

A relative newcomer to the e-shopping world, a Bill Me Later service works especially well for those customers who for some reason can't or won't use credit cards to shop online, or simply prefer an alternative to using credit.

A service of this nature is backed by a company that pays you, the merchant, for the customer's order. The customer registers with such a company and when approved for purchasing (approval is usually based on a credit check) he or she can make Bill Me Later purchases.

You as the merchant have very little to do with the transaction process – all you provide is a way for the customer to choose the Bill Me Later payment option on your site (Figure 2.14). Once the customer clicks the Bill Me Later option, he or she enters their password for their Bill Me Later provider. The provider pays you, the merchant, within a set period of time (usually two weeks). Then the purchasing company bills the customer directly.

Bill Me Later Service Providers

▶

Bill Me Later services are in use by a number of companies. Setting up service is different depending upon the provider you choose. The premiere providers at present include:

I4 Commerce (Developers of the Bill Me Later concept)

i4commerce.com

CyberSource cybersource.com/home.html

Paymentech paymentech.net

2.15

The main advantages of a Bill Me Later option are really for you, the merchant. It's a low-cost solution, and it takes a lot of the fear of fraud out of the process. On the other hand, the main advantage to customers is that they don't have to use a credit card for online transactions. However, since they still have to provide personal information to the provider, there is some sense that Bill Me Later services will have very limited use.

Cash-Based Transactions

Still another form of alternative payment options is the cash-based transaction. With this option, the customer opens an account with a cash-based provider. One such provider is RocketCash, rocketcash.com (Figure 2.15). These types of accounts have proven very popular with younger people as well as those persons preferring to use cash-based options.

The customer opens an account, which is free. Cash is added to the account via credit card, cheque, or money order, or by using promotional points, which are available at participating merchants. The customer can then make purchases at supporting merchant sites. Merchant implementation of this process will vary greatly, depending upon the provider you use.

> **NOTE**
>
> A list of digital cash transaction providers can be found at div2000.com/resources/referencesites/site.asp?groupid=19. This list includes digital cash opportunities for merchants and customers worldwide.

2.15 RocketCash is popular with younger online customers, **ROCKETCASH.COM**.
2.16 Offering cash options to customers can expand your customer base.

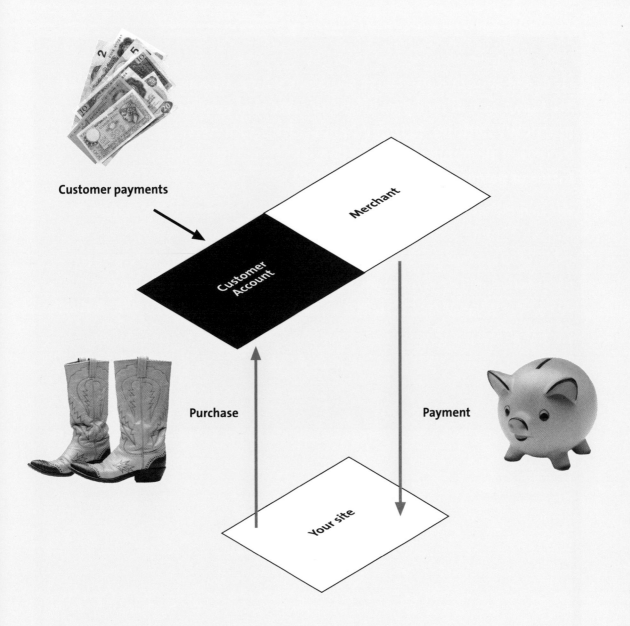

Managed Solutions

Managed solutions are those solutions where all transaction services are taken care of by a provider. The merchant does nothing, or practically nothing, to implement entire e-commerce solutions including shopping carts (see Chapter 3), credit card and other forms of payment processing.

The main disadvantage of a managed solution is the cost. Typically, managed solutions are almost as costly (and sometimes more) than dealing with standard merchant accounts. However, they are usually hassle-free. As the merchant, you don't do much more than pay the bill and your customers are provided with secure, convenient shopping on your website.

For more information about e-commerce managed solutions providers, see the Resources section at the end of this book.

Coming up next:

By now, you should have a good idea of the various options available for you when offering sales online. But to effectively organise inventory and make the shopping experience a pleasant one for your site visitors, shopping carts are really important – particularly when you have numerous items available on your site. In the next chapter, you'll learn about the various do-it-yourself, as well as managed options for shopping cart implementation.

3

SHOPPING CART SOLUTIONS

▶

If you're intending on having more than a handful of products on your storefront website, you're going to need help organising and maintaining the products and make it easy for people to shop comfortably. The solution is what is known as a "shopping cart".

Shopping carts are an interesting phenomenon because they appeared quite early in the web's life. Early shopping carts may in fact be the first complex application beyond simple form processing. For that reason, there are hundreds, if not thousands of shopping carts, spanning application types, cost, and management methods.

A SHOPPING CART IS AN APPLICATION THAT COMBINES WITH A DATABASE IN ORDER TO MANAGE THE SELECTION AND CHECKOUT PROCESS OF AN E-COMMERCE WEBSITE.

I think of shopping carts as falling into one of three main categories:

1. Free and Low-Cost Solutions

Typically, these are open source solutions, meaning that the shopping cart has been written using open source languages such as Perl or PHP. But, there are many in this category that use proprietary technologies but are still very low-cost as much of the installation depends upon you. These types of shopping carts can be excellent choices for the real do-it-yourselfer willing to take the time to manage the more complicated set-up, testing, and configuring of the program for your specific needs. Bear in mind there are many, and not all of them are going to be good, secure, or the most practical to install. Typically, if you are searching online for a good shopping cart solution of this nature, look for reviews and commentary from other people who have used the software before.

2. Hosted Solutions

As with the e-commerce accounts discussed in Chapter 2, there are managed solutions offered by host providers. Very often, the hosted solutions are offered by the same providers offering merchant accounts and order processing, so it can be very advantageous to use these "out-of-the-box" style solutions to manage your shopping cart needs with very little hassle. Of course, these solutions will cost, but typically not as much as custom software.

3. Custom Solutions

A custom solution is one that is built for your specific needs by a programmer. There are many applications and programs in which shopping cart software can be built for the web. Most readers will not opt for this because it can be both expensive and take time. However, if you are really going for a very highly custom site, with needs that might not be met by free, low-cost, or hosted options, a custom solution may well be something to consider.

3.1 A search at **SCRIPTSEARCH.COM** returned seven categories of information, with nearly 200 shopping cart options.

3.2 **4CHECKOUT.NET** offers a very affordable hosted shopping cart that's been highly rated as being effective, easy to use, and customisable.

Shopping Cart Design Guidelines

No matter which solution you end up using, there are certain important guidelines to follow when thinking about the interface of your shopping cart. If you are purchasing services, compare their options to these guidelines to ensure the greatest success.

– A shopping cart should always be referred to in the design as it reduces confusion for the user.

– Labels on buttons should make sense. For example, instead of a "BUY" button that really just adds the item to the cart, be sure to say "ADD" to avoid confusion for the consumer.

– Look for the fewest steps necessary for the shopping process. A user shouldn't have to go through tons of pages or constantly click a button to update his or her cart. The simpler and faster, the better.

– Shopping carts should acknowledge when an item has been added.

– Avoid shopping carts that make a user register prior to using the cart.

– Ensure that items can be quickly deleted as well as added.

– Final costs should be calculated by the software and displayed to the user prior to his or her entering any personal and/or credit card information.

3.3 The shopping cart at Red Envelope is cleanly designed and fits seamlessly into the rest of its interface, **REDENVELOPE.COM.**

Welcome to RedEnvelope.

*red*ENVELOPE

OCCASION   RECIPIENT   LIFESTYLE   SHOPS

my account • catalog request • shop our catalog • customer service • shopping bag

SEARCH product or item [go] refined search

SPECIAL OCCASIONS:

▸ summer sale
▸ grandparents' day (sep. 7)
▸ birthday
▸ wedding
▸ new baby
▸ just because
▸ more...

Or shop by:

▸ recipient
▸ lifestyle
▸ shops

We've got a gift for birthdays.

Getting older has its rewards. Make the most of their big day with an exceptional gift from our Birthday collection.

gift certificates • gifts by the month • corporate gifts • express gifts • catalog quick order • email sign-up

order tracking • about RedEnvelope • contact us • privacy policy • shipping

▶

Free and low-cost solutions are excellent choices for those individuals who aren't afraid to jump into what might on occasion be a complicated configuration adventure.

Open source solutions offer many advantages including:

- Huge selection of shopping cart types

- Available in many programming and application technologies including Perl, PHP, Java, ASP, ColdFusion, and CGI

- More customisation opportunities

- Available for a wide range of platforms (Windows, Unix, Linux)

- Free or low cost – most open source shopping cart solutions are priced at or below £150

- Typically, open source software has very accessible online support from enthusiasts as well as professional programmers

- You can try out a few different shopping carts without making a large financial commitment

Some of the disadvantages of open source shopping carts include:

- Possible complicated installation

- May require some knowledge of a programming or application language to help modify and customise the shopping cart

- May be simplistic in interface design and require design knowledge on your part to complete the design

- Inconsistent support options

You'll also want two general prerequisites:

- At least some familiarity with HTML

- Access to technical support via your service provider, systems administrator, or online programming forum

3.4

3.4 The sites shown above and opposite all use open source software; **HTTP://.EZ.NO**, **STUDIOA.US**, **THEKITCHENSHOP.COM**, **THEMAGICFLUTE.COM** and **SISTERSKY.COM**.

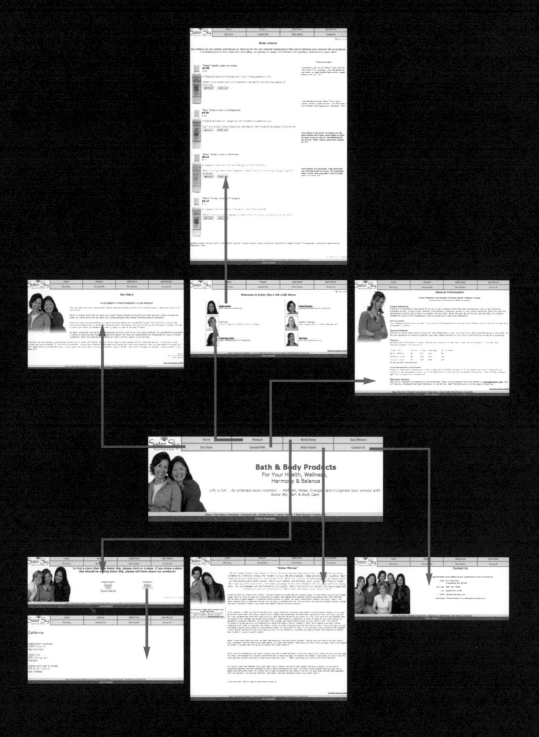

Open source software provides low cost or even free alternatives to higher-cost options, yet the shopping process will appear seamless to your customers. The main challenge with open source software is that it tends to demand more technical knowledge to work with than higher-cost but easy-to-implement solutions.

SHOPPING CART SOLUTIONS

Shopping Around

3.5

There are so many options and variables when it comes to choosing the correct shopping cart software for your needs that it's impossible to choose one for you. What's more, the installation and configuration of shopping carts can, as mentioned, be quite complicated.

While free and low-cost solutions require you to know or learn a bit about the programming language and platform available for your website needs, this is not to say that you have to sit down and actually learn the languages involved. You may have to learn a little just to get the customisation and configuration features done, and you certainly cannot have any fear of programming languages if you'd like to use free or low-cost services with any success. But, you do not have to become a programmer – just be familiar enough with the tools you'll be using in order to use them well.

Here are some steps you can take to determine what you have, what you need, and how to get started using a free or low-cost shopping cart solution.

> **NOTE**
> If you don't have an ISP, you can look for one in the Resource list provided at the end of this book.

1

Step 1. Survey the Services Available from Your ISP

The first thing you'll want to do is go to your ISP and find out what services are available for you. For the person who is going to be setting up a free or low-cost shopping cart, knowing the technology available is the first step toward finding the right solution.

Shopping carts come in a variety of programming and scripting languages, and depending upon the language used, will run on different server platforms including Unix, Linux, and Microsoft web servers. Most programming languages can run on all servers, but naturally there are restrictions depending upon the technology involved. Your ISP will help you make a decision regarding platform, and very often ISPs offer a choice of service packages with different platforms and languages available for your use.

3.5 Sample icons used throughout the web to symbolise shopping carts.

◀◀

Each shopping cart's language is going to offer different features. Along with a good database (SQL, MySQL, Oracle), you'll want to know which application language is available on your server. This will help you refine your shopping cart decision.

Typically, your ISP will have at least one of the following available:

Perl / CGI   **PHP**   **Java**   **ColdFusion**   **ASP / .NET**

Each of these programming languages offers the motivated reader different levels of challenges and benefits, as follows:

Perl / CGI. Perl is an extremely powerful, open-source programming language that allows for very detailed levels of customisation. CGI is a common gateway interface, and is used in tandem with Perl scripts to pass information back and forth between the site visitor's browser (client) and the web server. However, using Perl and CGI can be confusing for many and is likely not the best choice for a complete web design novice. There are many, many Perl-based shopping carts available, and most of them are free or very low cost.

TIP

Often, an ISP will offer more than one technology for a specific service package. This is especially true in the case of Perl and PHP. If you have the option, all the better, because you can try out a few different things and see which works best and is most comfortable for you.

3.6  **3.7** **3.8**  **3.9**

PHP. PHP is an easy-to-understand open source language that can be used for a range of website programming needs. There are quite a few shopping carts in PHP, and PHP is in general an excellent choice for the relative novice who has the time and inclination to work with it. PHP shopping carts are likely to be easy to install and maintain, as well as being free and very low cost.

Java. Java is a proprietary programming language by Sun Microsystems. It is best known for its cross-platform compatibility, making it useful on all kinds of operating systems. Many shopping carts are written in Java, but typically Java requires a high-level of knowledge to work with. Java shopping carts will also tend to cost more than those written in Perl or PHP.

ColdFusion. ColdFusion is an application language that is in general quite easy for anyone who has ever worked with HTML to use. This means a shopping cart written in ColdFusion will be fairly easy to configure, modify, and customise. ColdFusion is proprietary, but not as costly as Java. Also, it might not be the best choice if you think you will be growing into a very large operation, because ColdFusion is felt not to be as scalable as other solutions. Still, its ease of use makes it an attractive choice for many.

ASP / .NET. ASP technologies are proprietary Microsoft solutions. There is a range of very fine shopping cart solutions written in ASP. Typically, these will be fairly straightforward to set up and configure, but also likely to be a bit more on the expensive side.

3.6 The logo for Perl.
3.7 The PHP logo.
3.8 The logo for Java.
3.9 The ColdFusion logo.
3.10 The ASP logo.

3.10

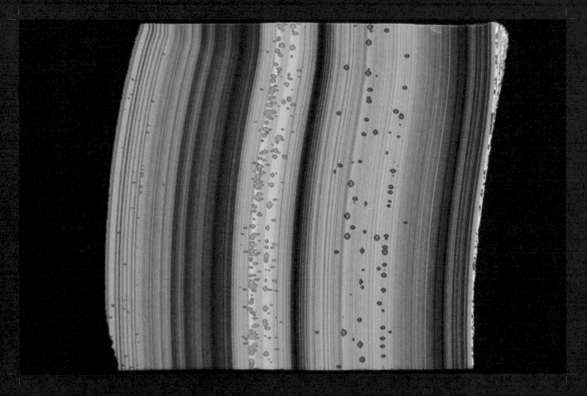

3.11 Screenshots from 1976 Design Photography,
1976DESIGN.COM/PHOTOGRAPHY.

Unable to find a shopping cart to meet his needs, site developer and photographer Dunstan Orchard decided to build his own.

Orchard is particularly concerned that his site and its shopping applications make the user experience a happy one. "My major tip in writing (or modifying existing) shopping carts is to be as helpful as you can to the user. Provide clues and tips wherever you think there might be confusion, preview buttons on order forms, names and phone numbers where people can complain, or the display of prices in multiple currencies."

Step 2. Search for Available Shopping Cart Software

Once you've ascertained the available technologies, you'll want to begin a search for shopping cart software. This is the hard part, because there are so many from which to choose – even though you've narrowed your options down by choosing a technology.

3.12

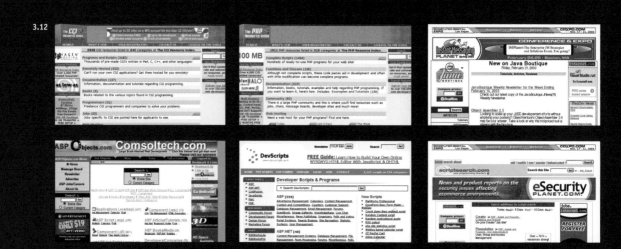

3.12 The programming and scripting resources shown here include **CGI.RESOURCEINDEX.COM**, **PHP.RESOURCEINDEX.COM**, **JAVABOUTIQUE.INTERNET.COM**, **ASPOBJECTS.COM**, **DEVSCRIPTS.COM** and **SCRIPTSEARCH.COM**.

Fortunately, there are excellent programming and scripting directories that you can use to search and, in many cases, try out shopping carts of different kinds. Here are a few helpful resources to get you started:

CGI Resource Index CGI.RESOURCEINDEX.COM

Here, you'll find plenty of CGI and Perl scripts, with shopping carts as well as documentation and additional Perl-related resources.

PHP Resource Index, PHP.RESOURCEINDEX.COM

Sister site to the CGI Resource Index, here you'll find plenty of PHP scripts, documentation, and reference materials.

Java Boutique, JAVABOUTIQUE.INTERNET.COM

Java applets, tutorials, and free Java source code.

ASPObjects.com, ASPOBJECTS.COM

This site offers a lot of free stuff, including shopping carts and other e-commerce related items.

DevScripts, DEVSCRIPTS.COM

Devscripts is an excellent place to look for numerous scripting and programming types including ASP, ColdFusion, Perl, and PHP.

Scriptsearch.com, SCRIPTSEARCH.COM

A vast resource for scripts, with annotated entries. There's a broad range of shopping carts here, available by language.

◀◀

3

Step 3. Download and Install the Programs

Once you've made a choice, you'll need to download the program. If there's a charge associated with your shopping cart, follow the provider's instructions as to purchase. Download the software to your local drive.

At this point, you'll need to use the documentation provided with the shopping cart to work through the installation process. Every program is going to be different, and again, some are going to be easier than others. The best tip I can offer for installation of free or low-cost shopping carts is to make sure that you have someone you can go to for help!

3.13

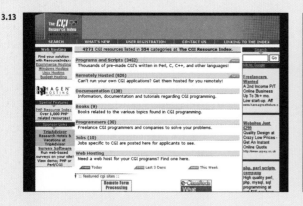
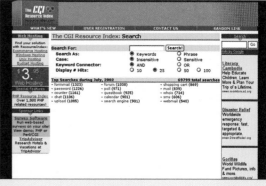

Fortunately, the resources provided in Step 2 will provide pointers to a community where someone with knowledge can in fact help you out. It's fairly common for programmers in general to spend at least part of every day assisting on lists and boards, helping people with exactly these issues. As noted earlier, this is especially true in open source communities such as with Perl and PHP, where the community spirit is very much alive.

3.13 At the CGI Resource Center, Perl shopping cart scripts are rated with comments, helping you to hone in on the best choice, **CGI-RESOURCES.COM.**

If the details of free and low-cost shopping cart solutions have got you flummoxed, and you're looking for a relatively inexpensive and hassle-free way of setting up a shopping cart, a hosted solution might just be for you.

Hosted solutions are those shopping cart services that are available from ISPs. They have several advantages, including:

– No decisions to make as to platform and software

– Hosted carts are pre-installed

– Configuration and customisation becomes the focus for you

– A hosted solution should have no hidden cost – your provider will tell you exactly how much you will be paying for the service, and a range of service options will likely be available

3.14

3.14 Examples of sites using hosted solutions include **FREAKSHOWART.COM**, **REFINEDLIVING.COM** and **CARVEL.COM**.

crit

Some of the disadvantages of hosted solutions include:

- Lack of control over shopping cart type and upgrades – you're dependent on the service provider to ensure that the product works and is updated with security patches and any other updates required

- While most services are reasonably priced, there will be ongoing additional costs associated with hosted solutions

- May mean major changes if you'd like to switch ISPs at a later date. Because the ISP is managing the cart and the technologies that drive it, you may have to reconfigure and even redesign your website if you make a switch to a different provider. This isn't true for free and low-cost solutions: If you have a Perl shopping cart running on a server and you decide to switch to a different ISP, so long

as Perl and any related technologies are enabled by that provider, you need only move your materials over to the new provider

Setting up a Hosted Solution

No doubt the biggest concern with hosted solutions is finding the right host for you. As with merchant accounts, whom you actually get the service from will make a great deal of difference in terms of security, stability, and customer service.

1

eria

If you'd like to use a hosted solution, you'll find the process easier if you follow these general steps:

Step 1. List Your Criteria

Planning is always key to a smooth journey. Before you begin your search for the right hosted solution, it's a good idea to list your criteria. Sit down, gather your website plans, and make a list that outlines the needs you have today, as well as those you foresee in the future.

Here's a sample list that I made:

Security The shopping cart must provide a high level of security

Flexibility The number of products I will have is going to change over time, so I need a lot of flexibility in how many products the shopping cart can handle

Ease of Use I want a shopping cart that is easy to manage and update

Customer Service Being able to rely on the ISP to fix problems or address concerns regarding my shopping cart service is critical

Scalability I'd like to be sure the ISP's hosted solution can grow with my commercial site

Foreseeing a Scalable Enterprise

Scalability in technology means the ability of that technology to scale according to the demands made upon it. For example, if you expect 30 visitors a day to make purchases from your site, when that number increases, the technology needs to be able to manage the additional demands smoothly and accurately.

It is essential for a shopping cart – or any e-commerce component for that matter – to be scalable. Part of the reason is that you expect your business to change and grow over time, both in volume and in product choice. Or, as with some e-commerce success stories, you may find that you suddenly come to a point where your business is catching on, and the demands on the technology must be seamless in order for you to have continued success. You always want to avoid server slow downs or shopping cart failures, or you'll lose the customer to someone else.

2

Step 2. Search for a Host

Once you have your list, you're off to the races. But, finding a host is easier said than done. Fortunately, many hosted solutions for your merchant accounts will also have shopping cart options attached. Check with your current ISP for their recommendations, as well as looking into those hosts mentioned in Chapter 2 and in the resources section of this book.

As with all Internet services, the location of your provider is unimportant. The thing you want to look for is stability and customer service. Check with the business agency local to the provider you choose to learn about the provider's consumer rating. Also, if many people have a problem with a service, you're likely to find that information online. However, go forth with caution! Many widely used services such as PayPal and Verisign have been publicly criticised for a variety of reasons, but still can be excellent service providers. Caveat Emptor!

3.15

Cheeta Technology Consulting	Sugar Land Texas United States
Clear Concepts Business Solutions	Winnipeg Canada
Computer Guy	Janesville Wisconsin United States
Computer Sisters, Inc.	Yelm Washington United States
Conexions Technologies	Surrey Canada
Connective Communications	Buena New Jersey United States
ConnectSharp.com	Houston Texas United States

3.15 SCRIPTSEARCH.COM provides a list of host providers.

▶▶

◀◀

3.16

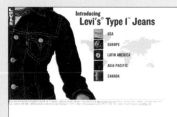

Step 3. Purchase Your Services

Seems obvious, I know. But if you buy your services online, it's fun to point out that you'll likely be using a shopping cart of some sort to make that purchase!

NOTE

An alternative to hosted solutions is a packaged solution. These are shopping carts that you buy – usually at a much higher price than free or low-cost solutions – and install yourself. The advantage here is that installation is very easy, and support is typically quite good. See the Resources section of this book for more information on packaged shopping cart solutions.

3

3.16 Sure, the big brands can afford custom solutions, but under the right circumstances they can work for smaller budgets too. Sites shown above include **NIKE.COM**, **GAP.COM**, **CARTIER.COM**, **AMAZON.COM** and **LEVI.COM**.

As mentioned in the introduction to this chapter, custom solutions can be very helpful in addressing certain needs that go beyond the scope of available and existing shopping cart packages. Or, perhaps you find a great option from the free and low-cost solution alternative, and you want to extend that program's ability.

A custom solution means that you hire a programmer to create a new shopping cart, or modify an existing one. There are certain very important advantages to this method:

– The shopping cart is completely customised to your needs

– The shopping cart can be designed for utmost security and scalability

– You'll have ongoing support from the programmer who develops your cart

Of course, there are some disadvantages to everything. In the case of a custom solution, the primary disadvantage is going to be cost. Custom solutions can be very expensive, and should be reserved for those situations where your business needs as well as your budget require them.

◀◀

Obtaining Custom Services

Finding the right programmer or team of programmers to develop your custom shopping cart is a major undertaking. Consider that not only do you want qualified people, but you also want to be sure that both the product and service you receive will meet your needs for the future as well as the present.

To undertake finding a good fit, follow these steps:

1. Prepare Yourself

Organise the following information:

– Who is your current ISP and what available technologies do they have? As with free and low-cost solutions, knowing which technology is available will help you figure out what kind of programmer you need

– Grab your list of requirements – this will help you express what it is you're looking for

– Understand and be prepared to explain why you are looking for a custom solution rather than using an existing option

2. Search for a Programmer

As with service providers, your programmer doesn't need to be local to you in order to provide you with excellent service. You're going to want to look for the programmer's website, and check out his or her work and references. Often, programmers or programming teams providing custom solutions of this nature have that kind of information available online.

To ferret out programmer resources online, you can do a broad search using Google or any other search engine and type in 'custom shopping cart solutions'. You'll find numerous entries and can research at will. Another option is to advertise on programming-related employment sites such as Elance, elance.com or freelance.com.

3.17 Elance provides services to help match you to a qualified programmer, **ELANCE.COM**.

3.18 Searching for a programmer on **FREELANCE.COM** is easy and fast.

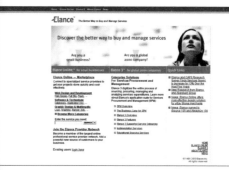

Finding technical assistance for your site is a breeze using websites such as elance and freelance.com. The important thing is to do your research first – know exactly what you are looking for! This will help you make a match between your needs and the best person for the job.

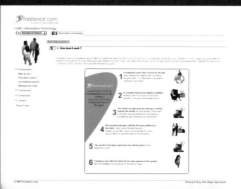

3. Prepare Your Potential Programmer

Once you've contacted a programmer suitable for your needs, if you come to the table with information in hand, you stand a much better chance of making your needs clear from the get-go and establishing a good relationship with your programmer right away. Often, the more information you can provide your programmer with, the better he or she can serve you both in terms of product and price. Take the information you've organised and talk to your programmer, but also be prepared to listen. He or she will provide you insight and helpful information that will allow you to make the best decisions regarding your custom application.

3.19

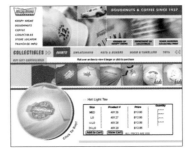

3.19 Screenshots from Krispy Kreme show how its website carries its whimsical image through all pages of the site, even in the shopping cart, **KRISPYKREME.COM.**

Topics covered:

Shopping cart solutions

Free and low-cost solutions

Hosted solutions

Custom solutions

Coming up next:

By now you not only have an idea of how to design an e-commerce website, but you also know what it takes to manage transactions as well as products. But once your site is up and running, how do you enhance it to make it more attractive to potential clients and customers? In the next chapter, you'll learn about a variety of e-commerce products that are both fun and useful for both you and your site visitors, as well as plenty of information to adequately promote your site.

Topics coming up next:

Business site promotions

Search and ye shall find

Email-based advertising

Advertising and product offerings

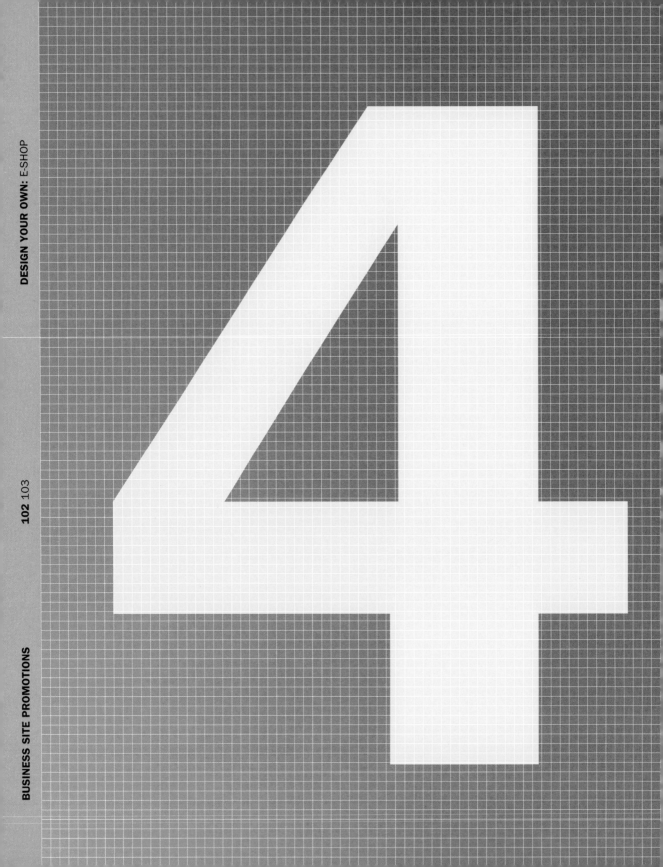

BUSINESS SITE PROMOTIONS

▶

While learning to customise your site for its audience, adding a merchant account, and adding a shopping cart are all important aspects of putting together a great e-shop, adding promotions and marketing are a necessary part of your site's success.

Whether you intend to use your website as an addition to your offline business, to provide products or services, or as a forum for your expression, you have to put some effort into marketing it. With the millions of web pages available today, your content could be lost and, as great as your site is, it might never get seen.

WITH THE MILLIONS OF WEB PAGES AVAILABLE TODAY, YOUR WEBSITE MUST BE MARKETED EFFECTIVELY IN ORDER TO STAND OUT.

There are several important means of promoting websites:

- Using search engines to improve your rankings

- Using email campaigns and newsletters to announce your site and any site-related events

- Working with banner ads

- Using offline and other marketing techniques such as promotional items

With so much commercialism on the web, it didn't take long for the advertising and marketing firms to step into the act – first to use a website as an advertising medium, and now recognising that many websites are not simply the means to a product but the product itself.

4.1

4.1 Pop-up ads are a popular method of trying to capture an online viewer's attention.

Search engines and directories can be powerful online marketing tools, but you must first understand how they work and how to best use them.

Search engines search the web on their own, finding web pages to add to their databases of listings.

Directories allow you to submit your web pages within categorised listings.

Google is a great example of a search engine, while Yahoo! perfectly exemplifies a directory.

4.2

4.3

4.2 Google is a popular search engine,
GOOGLE.COM.
4.3 Yahoo! is a long-running directory, broken down into topic areas,
YAHOO.COM.

Search Engines & Directory Listings

There are hundreds of search engines and directories, some appealing to very specific audiences. The most popular search engines appeal to a broad audience and have an easy-to-use interface.

Some of the more popular or well-liked search engines include:

Yahoo! yahoo.com
AltaVista altavista.com
Excite excite.com
Lycos lycos.com
HotBot hotbot.com
Infoseek infoseek.go.com
Dogpile dogpile.com
Google google.com

4.4 Screenshots of the search engines and directories listed above.

There are three ways you can get your site listed with a search engine or directory:

- Wait for search engines to find their way to your site.

- Submit your site to the search engines and directories with which you want to be listed.

- Use a listing service or software, usually for a fee.

Of course, being proactive and preparing your pages for search engines, directories, and even site listing services should you choose to use them, means preparing your documents for listing and ranking.

4.5

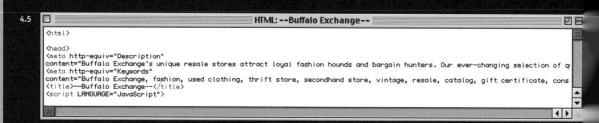

Improving Rank with Meta, Key Text, and Title

Engines use several primary methods to rank web pages: the text content of the page and the information provided via the meta element's attribute values.

Investing some time in the use and placement of keywords within the text of your document and in your meta elements can improve your chances of a high rank. What's more, how you title your page can make a difference, too.

Here, you'll learn to do both.

There are many types of uses for the meta element. The two we're most concerned with here are the meta element attributes used to provide description and keywords.

The meta element is placed in the head portion of your document. If you examine the legal-index.html file you worked with in Chapter 1, and look toward the top of the document, you'll see an opening HTML tag:

```
</head>
```

Your meta elements can be placed anywhere between this opening tag and its companion closing tag:

```
</head>
```

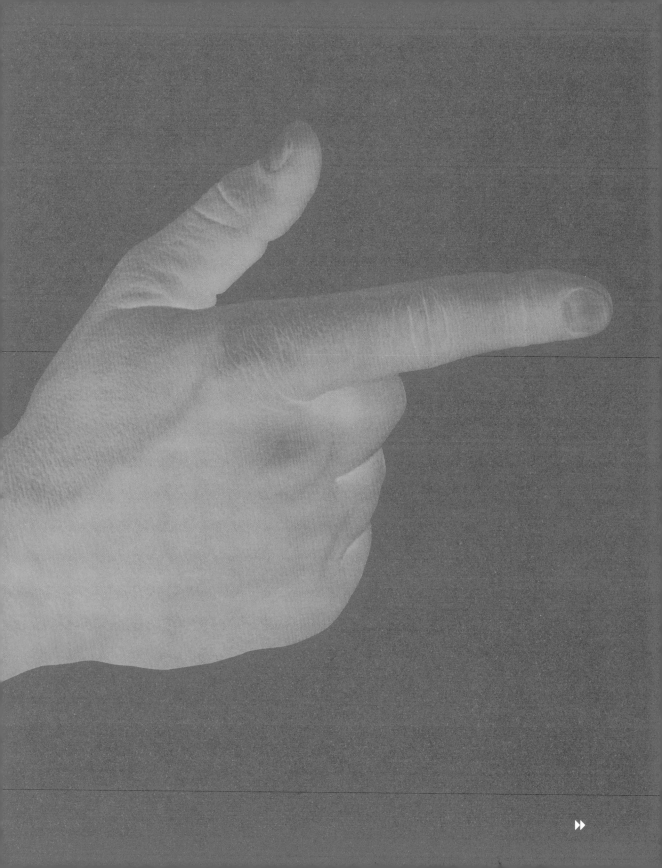

◀◀

To add your meta description and keywords to a page, follow these steps:

Enter the description code

Directly in your page, using your text or HTML editor, type in the following code:

```
<meta name="description" content=" ">
```

Enter the description into the content section

Enter your description into the empty quotation marks next to the word "content". Your description should be 25 words or less, and should clearly define what your website and goal is about.

An example might be:

Molly's Flowers is a warehouse flower shop in Tucson, AZ, offering high-quality, low-cost fresh flowers to vendors and individuals.

So, my results would look like this:

```
<meta name="description" content="Molly's
Flowers is a warehouse flower shop in Tucson,
AZ, offering high-quality, low-cost fresh
flowers to vendors and individuals.">
```

This way, when engines find my site, they can grab this information and use it as a description within their listings.

Enter the keyword code

The meta tag for keywords looks just like the markup used to define the description, only here the attribute is keywords:

```
<meta name="keywords" content=" ">
```

Prepare the keywords

Now, you'll add the keywords into the content portion of the code. There are quite a lot of things to remember when working with keywords. First, a comma should separate each word or string of words. Then, you must consider your keywords carefully, trying to imagine the experience a potential site visitor has when trying to find your product or service.

For example, a site visitor will undoubtedly come up with thousands of results if he or she enters "flowers". But if a user was looking for a flower shop in Tucson, he or she might type "Tucson flower shops".

It's to your benefit to include as many combinations of keywords as possible, and seek out those words which might not be as obvious, such as choosing to use specific flower types instead of just the word "flowers" in your keyword section. Unlike your descriptions, which should be kept to 25 or less, you can have as many keywords as you like (within the limitations of the engine or directory in question). It is also wise to include common misspellings in your keywords and international spellings of words like colour.

▶▶

Sitting down and preparing a long list of keywords prior to adding them to your page is a good idea. In fact, you may wish to work on this over a period of days, as you'll undoubtedly come up with new and useful keywords for your site.

5

Enter the keywords

Now that you've got a list of keywords, you'll want to add them to the code. Simply copy and paste the keywords from your list, directly in between the quotation marks surrounding the content.

Here's a short but accurate possibility:

```
<meta name="keywords" content="flower, rose,
chrysanthemums, dahlia, iris, tucson, arizona,
flower store, flower shop, flower shoppe,
warehouse flowers, fresh flowers">
```

With your meta information at the ready, a few other things to do to ensure better ranking include:

Repeat keywords within the early text content of your pages. Prominent keywords are weighted higher than words or phrases that occur near the bottom of the page, and some engines only read the first 200 words of a web page.

Name your documents clearly. Keep keywords in mind when naming your HTML documents. If a user is searching for information on Roses, **MOLLYSFLOWERS.COM/ROSES.HTML** will get a higher rank than **MOLLYSFLOWERS.COM/R.HTML**.

Giving your pages an appropriate title not only makes good design sense, but the title is also used by search engines and can increase the rank of your page if it includes the keywords. As with the meta element, the title element goes within the head portion of the document, and simply requires a good description of the site and page:

```
<title>Molly's Flowers: Caring for Your
Roses</title>
```

Buffalo Exchange, fashion, used clothing, thrift store, second-hand store, vintage, resale, catalogue, gift, certificate, consignment, retro, shop, costume, clothes, trade, sell, labels, recycled, trendy, clubwear, budget, style, glam, bargain, urban, funky, teen, young, hip, alternative

molly

molly.com

www.molly.com

molly holzschlag

window

hafsa

molly cam

cool web sites using perl

holzschlag

http//molly.emailers.org

livemotion molly

molly pics

molly veliffera

molly.com/pix

adobe pagemill png

colonial bakeries

jason and molly

kat meyer

Finding the right combination of keywords is not a science. It is impossible to predict exactly what someone will type into a search engine when looking for information on your product or service. You can do some research into the habits of searches by doing a few simple things. Ask your friends and colleagues what they would type in while searching for your product or service. You could even sit them down at a computer and write down the words and phrases they use when they are actively searching.

What's more, your ISP may well offer server-tracking services where you can actually analyse the keywords people use to find your site. My site provides this service, as you can see in Figure 4.7.

4.7 Studying keywords that people input to reach my website.

Hundreds, if not thousands, of new pages are submitted to search engines daily. Even if you get a high ranking, you could get moved down in the relevancy by new pages that are submitted. This is why follow-up is so important. You should monitor your rank on a regular basis, evaluating and resubmitting if your rank falls.

If your site was listed but had a poor ranking, visit some of the sites that made the highest ranking and use your browser to view the description, keywords, and way in which the text was prepared. Compare their markup to that from your page and try to determine why their page was given a higher rank.

NOTE

An excellent site for detailed information on how search engines work, and how you can leverage your power, try searchenginewatch.com.

The breadth and depth of information at Aboriginal Art Online provides a complete experience for the site visitor. A site visitor can learn a great deal about Aboriginal Arts as well as make purchases. Providing rich information and plenty of free materials along with your product can turn customers into long-term clients, as well as en… web at large.

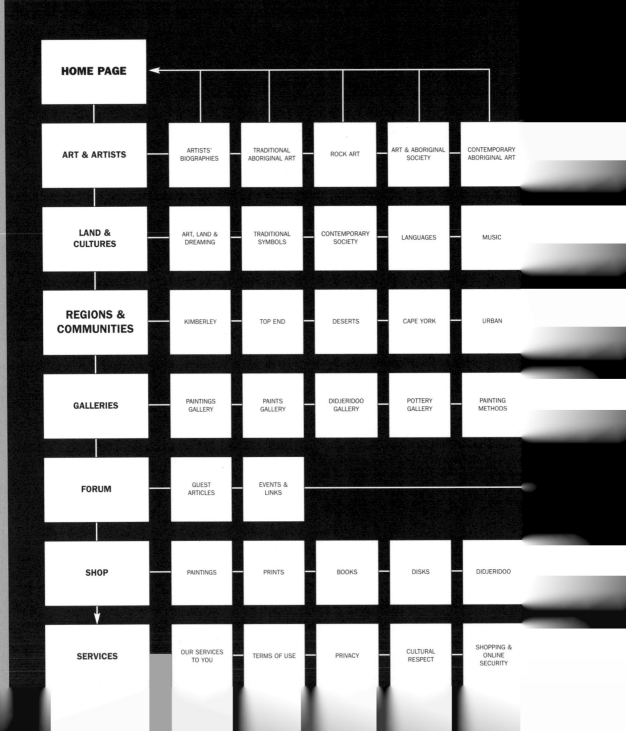

HOME PAGE					
ART & ARTISTS	ARTISTS' BIOGRAPHIES	TRADITIONAL ABORIGINAL ART	ROCK ART	ART & ABORIGINAL SOCIETY	CONTEMPORARY ABORIGINAL ART
LAND & CULTURES	ART, LAND & DREAMING	TRADITIONAL SYMBOLS	CONTEMPORARY SOCIETY	LANGUAGES	MUSIC
REGIONS & COMMUNITIES	KIMBERLEY	TOP END	DESERTS	CAPE YORK	URBAN
GALLERIES	PAINTINGS GALLERY	PAINTS GALLERY	DIDJERIDOO GALLERY	POTTERY GALLERY	PAINTING METHODS
FORUM	GUEST ARTICLES	EVENTS & LINKS			
SHOP	PAINTINGS	PRINTS	BOOKS	DISKS	DIDJERIDOO
SERVICES	OUR SERVICES TO YOU	TERMS OF USE	PRIVACY	CULTURAL RESPECT	SHOPPING & ONLINE SECURITY

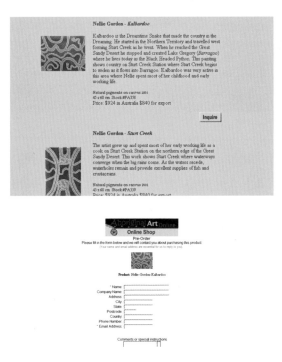

4.8 The Aboriginal Arts Online home page,
ABORIGINALARTONLINE.COM.

"Our marketing is mainly through making ourselves visible on the main online search engines under the main search terms people use to find Aboriginal art works," explains Martin Wardrop, Director of Aboriginal Arts Online.

Wardrop expresses a sense of success here, saying that there are now "...around 700 unique visitors per day on weekdays, with less on weekends."

According to Wardrop, the trick is "to convert visitors to sales!". He goes on to say, "We try to do this by encouraging interaction with customers, such as through individual email responses to inquiries." Wardrop also uses a regular newsletter to update interested visitors on items of interest.

Submissions Etiquette

As important as the preceding steps are to achieving a high ranking, there are some equally important things that you shouldn't do when preparing your pages for submission.

Avoid excessive repetition of keywords.

Unscrupulous personalities have sometimes intentionally overused keywords to gain the attention of sites. This is a form of abuse and should be avoided at all costs! If you repeat a keyword more than six or seven times, a red flag goes up at many search engines, and your page could be disqualified from the listing. It is also not a good idea to include popular keywords that don't have any relevance to your site.

Avoid multiple submissions of pages.

Many search engines have become extremely strict about how you list your pages. Overuse of keywords, inappropriate keywords for your site, and multiple attempts to submit the page are not only frowned on; they may render you disqualified from listing.

Use only your own trademarked names within keywords.

Playboy successfully sued the owner of an adult entertainment site that used the Playboy name in its meta tags to attract users to his site. Although the web has often had an aura of freedom, big business has been known to pay attention and crack down on trademark infringement.

Submitting Your Site

Now that you've defined your description, keywords, content, and title, it's time to get crackin'!

To submit your site, follow these steps:

Complete your Site!

Before submitting your site, make sure it is complete. With some engines taking weeks to list sites after submission, it may be tempting to submit your site before it is finished. This works in some cases, but many engines verify that your site is valid on the day of submission, and if they don't find your index or home page, your submission could be deleted.

Submit your URL

Submitting your site to be included in a search engine or directory database is remarkably easy. You simply go to the engine you are interested in and look for the "Submit URL" or "Add URL" button or link. You can usually find these at the bottom of the page (Figure 4.9).

4.9 URL submission link on AltaVista, **ALTAVISTA.COM**.

4.9

TIP

Read the search engine's submission guidelines carefully. Here, you'll find what you are allowed to do and what might be considered inappropriate use of the engine. Remember, search engine and directory listings of this nature are free! We don't want to abuse this powerful and beneficial means of promoting sites.

Most engines only require that you submit your home page, because they will seek out links on that page and go down two or three levels to find other pages to include in their database. It doesn't hurt to submit a few of your most important pages in addition to your home page. It is not advisable to submit every single page within your site. Many engines are taking a stand against people they feel are abusing their services. Some engines monitor the number of pages a person submits and often limit the number of pages you can submit in one day.

❸ Follow-up

After you have submitted your pages to the search engines you have selected, plan your follow-up. Each search engine has its own turn-around time. Some take only a few hours to list your page, although others can take up to six weeks. It is important to record these turn-around times and check back to see if your site was accepted. If your site has not been listed, you must resubmit it. Some search engines require that you email any resubmissions; record this next to the turn-around time.

4.10 Screenshots from the following sites: **FREEBORD.COM, ANNASUI.COM, BILLABONG.COM, THEWAYFARERS.COM** and **FLOWERBUD.COM.**

Buffalo Exchange: Keyword Strategy

" As part of our search engine strategy, we create a unique list of keywords and keyword phrases for each page," says Scott Burr, one of the programmers behind the website for Buffalo Exchange.

" The keyword lists are based on realistic search terms tailored to our audience and compiled from the actual page content to maximise their efficiency. Broad terms are avoided in favour of more focused phrases that reflect the primary topics for each page."

" When page content is significantly changed, we make sure to update the keywords as well. We find that this strategy helps us reach our intended audience by improving our page relevance within search results."

4.11

4.12

4.11 Feature stories are broken into short segments and can be "paged through", similar to a fashion magazine.

4.12 Locations lists the cities in which physical stores can be found. By highlighting a particular city the viewer can find out the exact address and other useful pieces of information such as opening times.

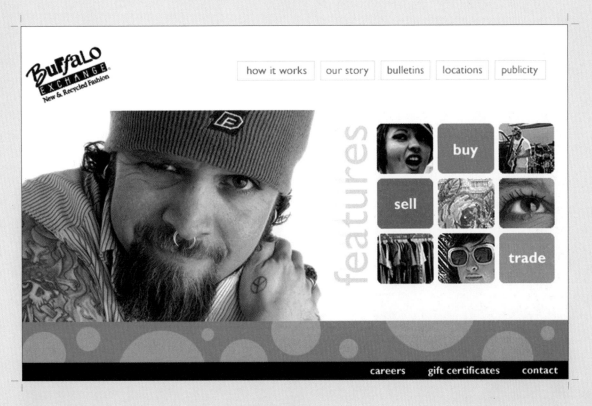

4.13 The home page of the site, showing a rollover treatment, **BUFFALOEXCHANGE.COM**.

4.14 Sample web pages.

Subscription Services

If listing your sites is too time consuming for you, you can subscribe to the commercial subscription services offered at listing services such as bCentral, bcentral.com.

These services submit your site to many search engines and directories, often charging different amounts for the type and/or number of search engines to which they submit your site, or offering free services along with subsidised advertising banners.

Although submitting your site is easy, it is not enough to make search engines an effective marketing tool. Unless your site is returned within the first two or three pages of listings, it may never be seen. The challenge when submitting your site is to improve your ranking.

4.15 bCentral service,
BCENTRAL.COM.

EMAIL-BASED ADVERTISING

Email is the number one reason people connect to the Internet. An email address is almost (if not more, for some people) as important as a phone number as a method of communication.

One of the most common ways email is used as a marketing tool is by unsolicited commercial emailing. This is similar to sending out flyers in the regular mail. It tends to be an extremely ineffective marketing strategy, as most people not only dislike but out and out resent spam.

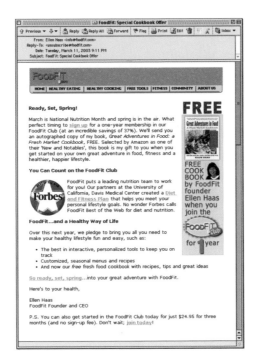

4.16 Email newsletters, if used on a subscription-only basis, can be a very effective means of online marketing.

Spamming is Not Acceptable

There's a huge difference between using email for marketing and using it for spam. Marketing email and news should always be at the discretion of the site visitor.

Spamming has such a negative reputation on the Internet that several organisations have been formed to fight it. The most noteworthy and international of these organisations is Cauce: Coalition Against Unsolicited Commercial Email, **CAUCE.ORG.**

Email users take great offense to receiving unsolicited advertising email, much more so than to receiving flyers with their local newspaper. If you were to send out bulk email, the response would be overwhelmingly negative and would not portray your business as trustworthy.

So, don't spam. But that shouldn't dissuade you from using email as a marketing tool; there are some respected and appropriate ways to do so:

Provide opt-in mail receiving options. You can do this by including the option on a form on your site, and very clearly explaining what it is the site visitor is going to receive (or not receive) in kind. You then have the permission of the recipient, and the promotional materials you send would not be considered unsolicited spam.

Make it easy for people to sign on or off your service. Always include an easy way for people to subscribe or unsubscribe to your notices, and provide information about other subscription options.

Use email-based news. Write a newsletter relating to the content on your site that can be sent to people who sign up on your website. If you had a site devoted to aspiring e-shop owners, you could send a weekly newsletter giving some insight into your experiences, perhaps a tip or two, pointing them to the website for more details and information. As with your product or services announcements, it is important to give the subscribers to your newsletter a clear and easy way to unsubscribe.

4.17 Spam fighting with Cauce, **CAUCE.ORG.**

◄◄

Never sell your email lists unless it is made very clear to your site visitors that you are doing so. No one likes to be signed up for things they don't want. I personally find this practice abhorrent anyway, because it sets up a chain of list selling where ultimately the recipient ends up receiving unwanted emails. But if you have to do it, I encourage you to do it very honestly, clearly, and with your site visitors' clear consent.

Another, very popular but rarely discussed way to garner more exposure for your site through email is to include a signature file with all your email correspondence (Figure 4.18).

4.18

Molly E. Holzschlag, Education Director
World Organization of Webmasters, http://www.joinwow.org/
personal site: http://www.molly.com/
molly@molly.com

TIP

Most email programs let you automate a signature that is placed automatically at the bottom of all emails you send out.
Be sure to keep them only to a few lines, and be sure also to include your website address, and your email address.
It's amazing how this virtual "word of mouth" can boost interest in your site.

▶

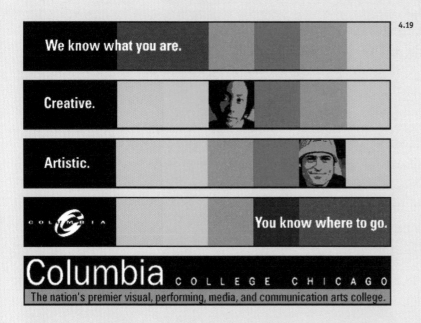

4.19

4.18 Email signature.

4.19 Using animation in banners can be an effective way to get users' attention.

Banner ads are the most common form of advertising on the web to date. It is rare to find a public site that doesn't include some form of banner ad somewhere within its pages. Banner ads offer a unique approach to advertising not found in print or offline marketing. How often in offline advertising can the reader be at your store within seconds of viewing the ad? With banner advertising, potential customers are virtually one mouse click from your product.

But banner ads have notorious problems, so you might choose not to use them at all. Whether you do or not, other things can enhance your marketing goals, so I'll be sure to include sidebars to point those options out to you.

More About Banners

▶

To better understand this popular form of online advertising, it is important to be familiar with some industry buzzwords.

Banner ad

This is a graphical advertisement, usually a GIF image and often animated. A very common industry size is 468 x 60 pixels, with weight between 5 and 10KB. However, new sizes have been emerging for the past several years, as have different kinds of banner ads.

Click-through

The number of people who click a banner ad and get to the advertiser's website.

Page impressions or page views

These terms refer to the number of visitors who view a page.

Flat fee

This is where a site owner charges you a flat fee per month for advertising on the site. This price structure is rare and is usually found on smaller sites.

CPM/Cost-per-Thousand

When paying for advertising through CPM, you are paying for how many times your ad is displayed each month. This is the most common type of payment structure, and many larger sites require that you purchase a minimum amount of impressions.

4.20 A sampling of some of the banner advertisements used online. These ads all follow the popular format of 468 x 60 pixels.

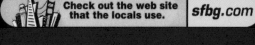

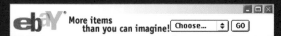

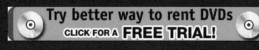

Alternatives to Banners

Put Your Logo Everywhere

If you want to help branding initiatives, invest some money in putting your logos on promotional items: Shirts, mugs, caps, mouse pads. You can find a local vendor to help you with this, or look online.

A very impressive site that can assist you with setting up a store for such items is cafepress.com. They offer a range of services from small businesses all the way to large corporate relationships.

4.21

Banner advertising can cost anywhere from thousands of dollars to no cost by using a banner exchange. There are a variety of price structures when dealing with paid advertising.

4.21 CaféPress makes it easy to put your logo on custom-designed products like t-shirts, mugs and other merchandise, **CAFEPRESS.COM**.

4.22 Although 468 x 60 pixel banner ads are still probably the most widespread, there are opportunities to place a variety of sizes in different online publications.

The two most popular pricing structures include:

By impressions. This is how many times the banner ad is actually seen onscreen.

By click-through. When a site visitor clicks on a banner ad to visit the advertised site, this is referred to as click-through.

For example, Yahoo!, the most popular search engine, has a 500,000 impressions minimum. This is a very high number of impressions per ad, making the impression rate structure very expensive. In terms of click-through rates, some sites charge you for how many people click your ad, not how many people see the ad.

4.22

1. PUT YOUR LOGO EVERYWHERE

DOES BANNER ADVERTISING ACTUALLY WORK?

Banner ads are an industry standard; you see them everywhere. But how often do you actually click one?

The industry average click-through rate is very low. Nielsen Netratings estimates as of July 2001 reflected 0.28% click through. That's not even 1%. If you have 100 site visitors to your site an hour, that's 1 click through. So where's the return on investment?

Some say the power of banner advertising is akin to the power of highway billboards, and it's an apt metaphor. As people pass a banner, the message and branding of a given company is expressed. After seeing so many along the way, the brand is remembered by the site visitor.

4.23

An alternative to high-priced banner placement is banner exchange. A banner exchange is a good way to experiment with banner advertising without involving the large cost of paid advertising. The concept behind an exchange is simple, you allow other members of the exchange to post their banners on your site, and, in return, your banner gets posted on the sites of other members.

The drawback is, of course, having a banner on your page that can pull a user away before he or she has seen your site. There are, however, many advantages to using a banner exchange. Some exchanges let you target specific sites; this is important in effective banner advertising. Some also offer a high ratio of exchange – you get two views for every one you display – and many will give you hundreds of "free" views for signing up.

There are numerous, maybe even countless banner ad exchange programs. Try Exchange It, exchange-it.com, or Global Banner Exchange, 1-2-free.com/banner/global, and do a search to your geographical location – there are banner exchanges based on regions, even cities! This can be a very good way to get attention for your business.

Many exchanges also give you extensive performance statistics, including page impressions and click-throughs. It might be a good idea to use a banner exchange to get a feel for their effectiveness before moving on to paid advertising.

4.23 Two examples of sites which offer banner ad exchange programs, **EXCHANGE-IT.COM** and **1-2-FREE.COM**.

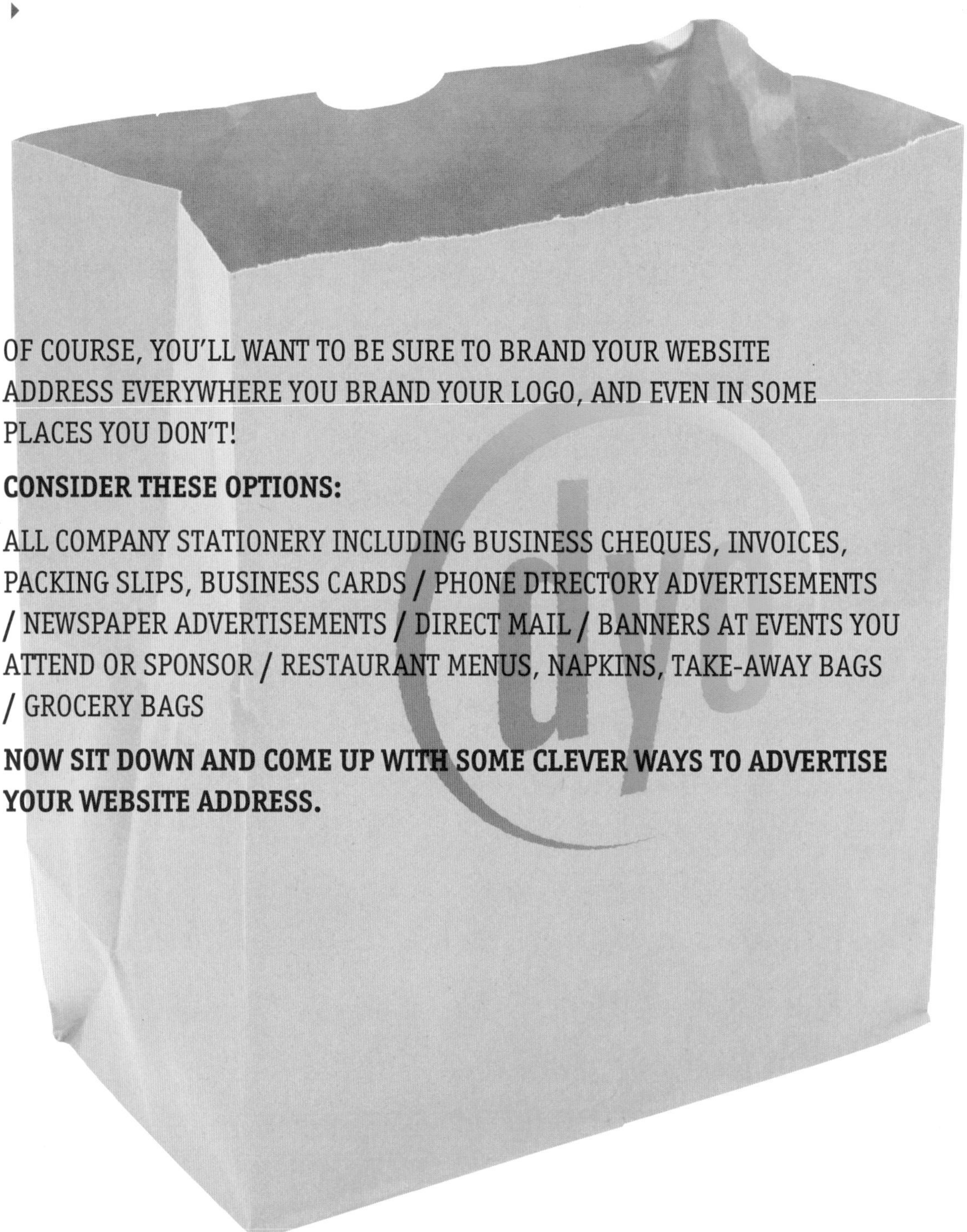

OF COURSE, YOU'LL WANT TO BE SURE TO BRAND YOUR WEBSITE ADDRESS EVERYWHERE YOU BRAND YOUR LOGO, AND EVEN IN SOME PLACES YOU DON'T!

CONSIDER THESE OPTIONS:

ALL COMPANY STATIONERY INCLUDING BUSINESS CHEQUES, INVOICES, PACKING SLIPS, BUSINESS CARDS / PHONE DIRECTORY ADVERTISEMENTS / NEWSPAPER ADVERTISEMENTS / DIRECT MAIL / BANNERS AT EVENTS YOU ATTEND OR SPONSOR / RESTAURANT MENUS, NAPKINS, TAKE-AWAY BAGS / GROCERY BAGS

NOW SIT DOWN AND COME UP WITH SOME CLEVER WAYS TO ADVERTISE YOUR WEBSITE ADDRESS.

success story:

It's hard to believe in four short chapters you've done so much. You've learned the basics of setting up a web page, you've got all the info you require about merchant accounts, hosting, shopping cart services and the marketing and promotions of your website.

But do stay aware – trends change, some services become more affordable and practical, design issues and user interest will fluctuate too. You have to remain vigilant to ensure that your website is fulfilling the needs of your audience. If you follow practical business guidelines and pay attention to the changing nature of the web, I've little doubt that your e-shop will be a success!

Now design your own site!

GLOSSARY

Alternative online payments: The use of payment methods not related to standard merchant accounts or hosted credit-card processing solutions.

ASP: Active Server Pages. ASP is a technology that typically runs on Microsoft web servers and can be used to help program effective shopping carts and other dynamic features of a website.

Client: The computer that requests the information.

ColdFusion: ColdFusion is an application's language that assists developers in creating tools such as shopping carts and transaction capabilities.

Compression: Any means of making a file smaller.

CSS: Cascading Style Sheets. A web language that works in tandem with HTML or XHTML to control the style and layout of web pages.

E-commerce: Electronic commerce. This is the concept of using electronic means to manage transactions.

FTP: File Transfer Protocol. This is an Internet-based technology that allows you to transfer files directly from your machine to a remote server.

FTP Client: A software program that lets you use File Transfer Protocol.

GIF: Graphic Interchange Format. A file format used on the web that is best suited for line art or art with few, flat colours.

GIF Animation: The use of the GIF format to create short animations.

Home Page: A personal web page; also used to refer to the default page found when a site loads.

HTML: Hypertext Markup Language. A language that marks up documents for the web.

Hypermedia: Text, images, or other media that when activated, allow another action to occur.

Hypertext: Text that is interactive and when activated, calls another action to occur.

Imaging Program: A software program that allows you to manipulate and create images.

Information Architecture: The structuring of information so that it is usable and navigable.

Interactivity: Allowing the user to interact with a given page or element within a page.

Interface: The features of a software program or website that allow a person to interact with it.

Interoperability: The ability of documents to be used no matter across platforms. See platform independence.

ISP: Internet Service Provider. This is a company providing Internet access as well as other Internet and web-based services.

Java: Java is a platform-independent programming language that is used for a wide range of applications, including shopping cart and secure transaction management.

JavaScript: A scripting language that you can use to add dynamic tools and interactivity to your web pages.

JPEG: Joint Photographic Experts Group. The JPEG file format for the web is best suited for photos and images with a lot of variation of light and colour.

Managed Accounts: Service providers that provide you with a complete transaction management solution.

Merchant Account: An account provided by a bank or other financial institution to help you manage credit card processing on your website.

Perl: A language which can be used for various aspects of behind-the-scenes management of websites. Many shopping cart technologies are written in Perl.

Persona: A persona is the creation of fictitious audience members that are then used to test sites for usability. These fictitious personalities are matched with aspects of the site: Language, colours, content, and navigation.

PHP: An open-source language that is used, like Perl, for a variety of behind-the-scenes site management. Many shopping cart technologies are written in PHP.

Platform: The various combinations of hardware and operating system software used for computers.

Platform Independent: The ability of software to run on any platform.

Secure Transaction: A transaction that utilises a variety of security methods and protocols in order to ensure the transaction is safe.

Server: A computer whose job it is to serve information as it is requested.

Shopping Cart: A shopping cart is an application that combines with a database in order to manage the selection and checkout process of an e-commerce website.

Site Map: An outline or schematic of your website's structure.

SSL: Secure Sockets Layer. The conventional method of securing online transactions.

Templates: A predefined design into which you can add your own elements.

Visual Editor: Software program that allows you to work visually while it generates the underlying markup and CSS.

WYSIWYG: What You See is What You Get. Another term for a visual editor.

XHTML: Extensible Hypertext Markup Language. The new generation of HTML.

RESOURCES

ISP & MERCHANT RESOURCES

The List
A master list of ISPs worldwide. Some of these providers offer a wide range of hosted and managed solutions, **THELIST.COM**.

Verisign
Out sources security and e-commerce solutions worldwide, and offers a line of products that can assist you with not only the security aspects of e-commerce, but also the payment processing as well, **VERISIGN.COM**.

PayPal
PayPal, **PAYPAL.COM**, is an extremely popular way for merchants and buyers to make quick transactions. PayPal requires both the merchant and the buyer to have a PayPal account.

Bill Me Later
Bill Me Later services are in use by a number of companies. Setting up a service is different depending upon the provider you choose. The premiere providers at present include: I4 Commerce (Developers of the Bill Me Later concept), **i4commerce.com**, CyberSource, **cybersource.com** and Paymentech, **PAYMENTECH.NET**.

Digital Cash
A list of digital cash transaction providers can be found at **DIV2000.COM/RESOURCES/REFERENCESITES/SITE.ASP?GROU PID=19**. This list includes digital cash opportunities for merchants and customers worldwide.

WEBSITES OF INTEREST

A List Apart
Run by Jeffrey Zeldman, A List Apart is a cutting edge magazine filled with tutorials and information about web design, **ALISTAPART.COM**.

Builder.com
C|NET's entry for web designers. Targets information on just about every aspect of web design. Vast resources, links, and great articles, **BUILDER.COM**.

Devhead
Ziff-Davis offers up this extremely content-rich developer's site. You'll find news, features, and a wonderful script library for Java applets, JavaScript, and Perl/CGI scripts, **DEVHEAD.COM**.

Hot Source HTML Help
A good source for all HTML help with a good section on DHTML, **SBRADY.COM/HOTSOURCE**.

The HTML Bad Style Page
I rather like it for the fact that it shows you what NOT to do with HTML. Sometimes it is nice to see a sample of poor workmanship to avoid it, **EARTH.COM/BAD-STYLE**.

Lynda.Com
Books, colour references, and plenty of wisdom from web graphics expert Lynda Weinman, **LYNDA.COM**.

Mark Radcliffe's Advanced HTML
Covering a variety of topics – includes helpful HTML hints. **NEILJOHAN.COM/HTML/ADVANCEDHTML.HTM**.

Microsoft Developer Network
An unbelievable variety of information covering web building and publishing. Lots of community, heavy on Internet Explorer-specific information, **MSDN.MICROSOFT.COM**.

The Sevloid Guide to Web Design

A collection of over 100 tips, tricks, and techniques on every aspect of web design, including page layout, navigation, content, graphics, and more. **SEV.COM.AU/WEBZONE/DESIGN.ASP.**

Web Designers Virtual Library (WDVL)

For years Alan Richmond put together one of the most accessible comprehensive resources for designers and developers. Now it's available via Internet.com. **WDVL.COM.**

Webmonkey

A well done, eye-pleasing page that has lots of tutorials and a great sense of humour, **WEBMONKEY.COM.**

Web Page Design for Designers

Explore the possibilities of web design from the standpoint of a designer, **WPDFD.COM.**

Webreference

Vast references, tutorials, and hints about web design, **WEBREFERENCE.COM.**

Yale C/AIM Web Style Guide

An excellent, straightforward overview of interface, site design, graphics, multimedia, and, of course, HTML. Now available as a book as well. **INFO.MED.YALE.EDU/CAIM/MANUAL/ CONTENTS.HTML.**

MAILING LISTS

Babble

Geared to advanced web design issues, and includes a lively exchange of information, resources, theories, and practices of designers and developers, **BABBLELIST.COM.**

WebDesign-L

WebDesign-L is a mailing list community created in early 1997. The list is intended as a forum for those involved in creating the web – whether for business, for self-expression, or for exploring the possibilities of a new medium, **WEBDESIGN-L.COM.**

ORGANISATIONS

The Web Standards Project: WaSP

Dedicated to providing information and a voice in promoting web standards, **WEBSTANDARDS.ORG.**

World Wide Web Consortium

Standard, standard, who's got the standard? W3C is the first stop for all advancing HTML and related technology students, **W3.ORG.**

The World Organization of Webmasters

Educational and peer-support resources for Webmasters, **JOINWOW.ORG.**

Association for Women in Computing

A general organisation for women in the computer field, **AWC-HQ.ORG.**

Webgrrls

The international networking group for women interested in the Internet. Multiple sites by country and city; start at the home page, **WEBGRRLS.COM.**